Building real life web apps with Angular 18 and ASP.NET Core 8

ISBN: 9798335849517

Copyright © 2024 by Haris Tsetsekas

Table of Contents

Introduction 5
1. Project setup 7
2. Product list and details page 11
3. Pagination 17
4. Product filtering 25
5. Cart functionality 31
6. Creating the ASP.NET Core 8 Web API 37
7. API pagination and frontend-backend integration 45
8. Authentication 51
9. Authorization 63
10. Authentication —Access token refresh/revoke 71
11. Checkout 79
12. Order validation and submission 91
13. Error handling and logging 109
14. User registration 121
15. Cart in local storage 143
16. Admin functionality 149
17. Order processing 167
18. Angular testing – part 1 177
19. Angular testing – part 2 187
20. ASP.NET Core Web API testing 199

Introduction

This book aims to help readers learn Angular 18 and ASP.NET Core 8 by developing step-by-step on a real-life project.

Let's see the main requirements for this project: The main purpose of the online store is to present users with a catalog of the products on sale. This catalog will provide the ability to search for text, as well as apply simple filters, such as product category. Users may insert the selected products in the cart and then proceed to checkout and submission of their order.

The web store will also enable administrators to modify the product catalog, by adding / editing / deleting products. Administrators will also be able to view submitted orders.

The web store will be open to anonymous users to browse through the catalog. Users will need to register in order to proceed with their purchase. Admin pages will be available only to authorized users.

In order to avoid unneeded complexity and at the same time highlight the important issues of Angular development, the web app will have a simple design. For instance, only the product name and its short description will be maintained, along with the product photo and price. Furthermore, we will not use a lot of CSS in this book, but Bootstrap will be employed in order to attain a simple but elegant design.

In contrast to the store design, its functionality will be far from rudimentary. It is the aim of the tutorial to use as many important capabilities of the Angular framework as possible. For instance, pagination will be used for the catalog main page and filters will appear as pop-up windows. Communication with the backend API will be authenticated via JSON Web Tokens (JWT). Moreover, routing and validation functionality will be used throughout the project.

On the backend side, the API will follow a REST-like approach, using the ASP.NET Core Web API functionality. As far as persistence is concerned, the Entity Framework (EF) code-first approach will be used, where the database tables are created by code, in a series of migrations.

Last but not least, the code will be accompanied by unit tests, where appropriate. This means that we will not try to reach large code coverage, but we will see targeted and detailed examples for each type of testing.

It should be noted that this is not an introduction to Angular, but a more advanced guide to the development of actual web applications with Angular. In order to be able to follow the course of the implementation, some familiarity with JavaScript or Typescript and Angular as well as C# would be necessary. A good place to start is the introduction to Angular at https://angular.dev/tutorials. So, let's get started with the project setup!

1. Project setup

We will need to have the following software installed in our development workstation:

- .Net 8 SDK (installed together with Visual Studio 2022)
- Node.js (the latest LTS version)
- Angular 18

After we download and install the latest LTS version of Node.js, we open a new Command Prompt and we install (globally) the latest Angular version:

```
npm install -g @angular/cli
```

With regard to IDEs, at least two good options are available: Visual Studio 2022 Community Edition, and Visual Studio Code. Both IDEs are free to use and provide amazing options to developers.

Our web application will consist of two separate projects, one for the frontend (the web site developed with Angular) and one for the backend (the API developed with ASP.NET Core).

One option would be to use Visual Studio 2022 and create a single solution containing two projects. Another option would be to have two separate projects for frontend and backend, created on VS Code and VS2022 respectively. For this tutorial, the first option will be selected.

When we start Visual Studio 2022, we are prompted to create a new solution. We will choose to create "*Angular and ASP.NET Core*" solution:

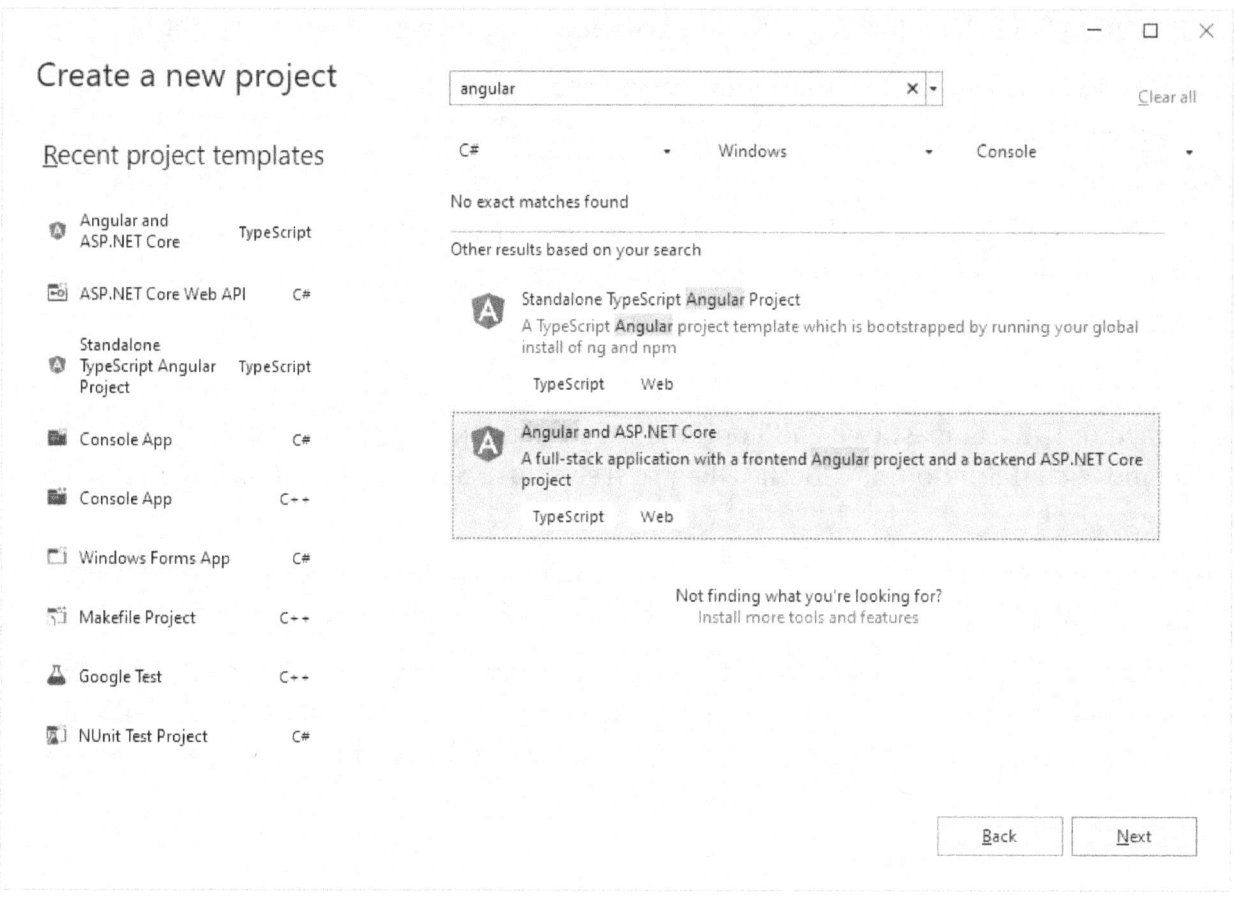

We give the name *eshop-angular-18* and we keep the default options in the last page:

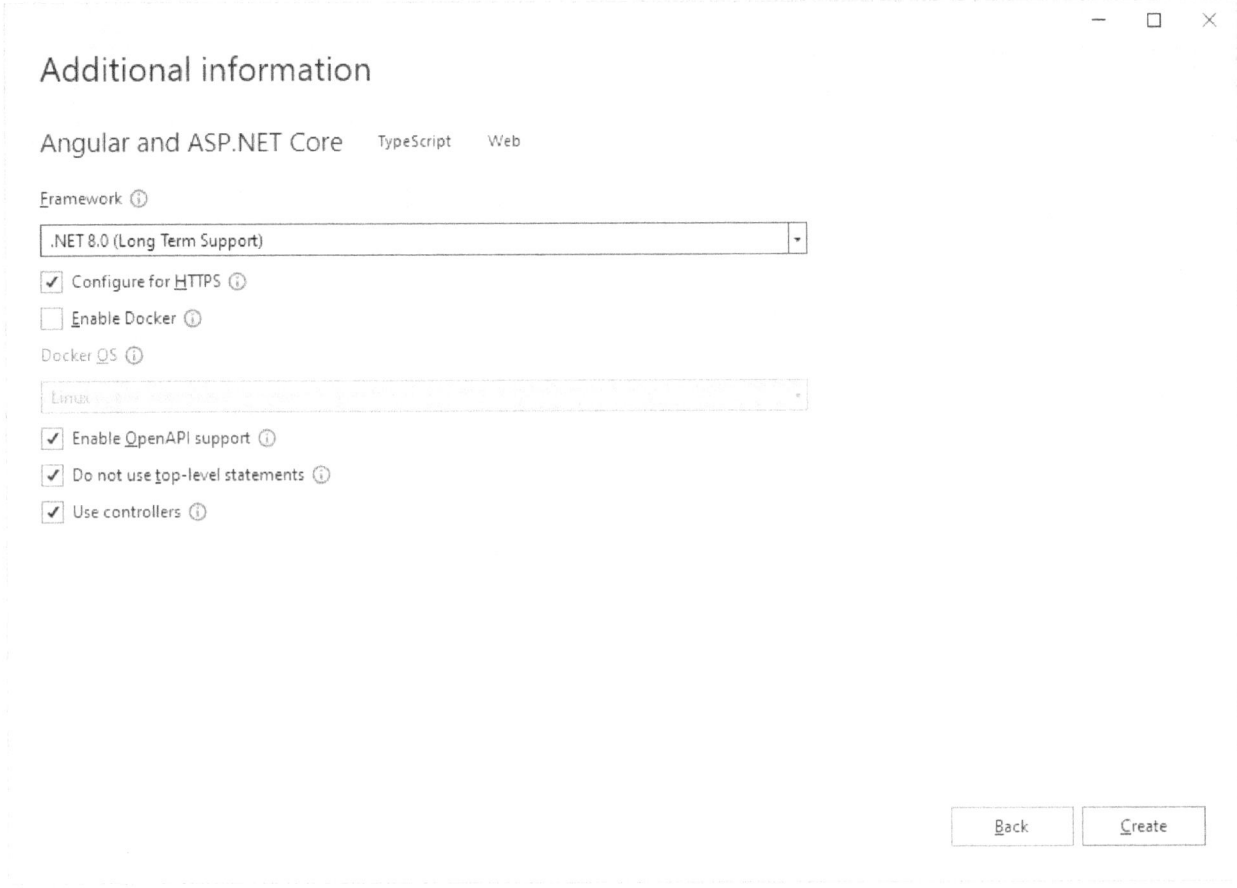

Version control

We will use Git for version control. We choose to create a common repository for both projects.

VS 2022 provides us with a nice wizard to create the repository as well as push it in our account in GitHub. It can also create a generic .gitignore file so as to avoid storing .obj files and all *node_modules* folders in our repository:

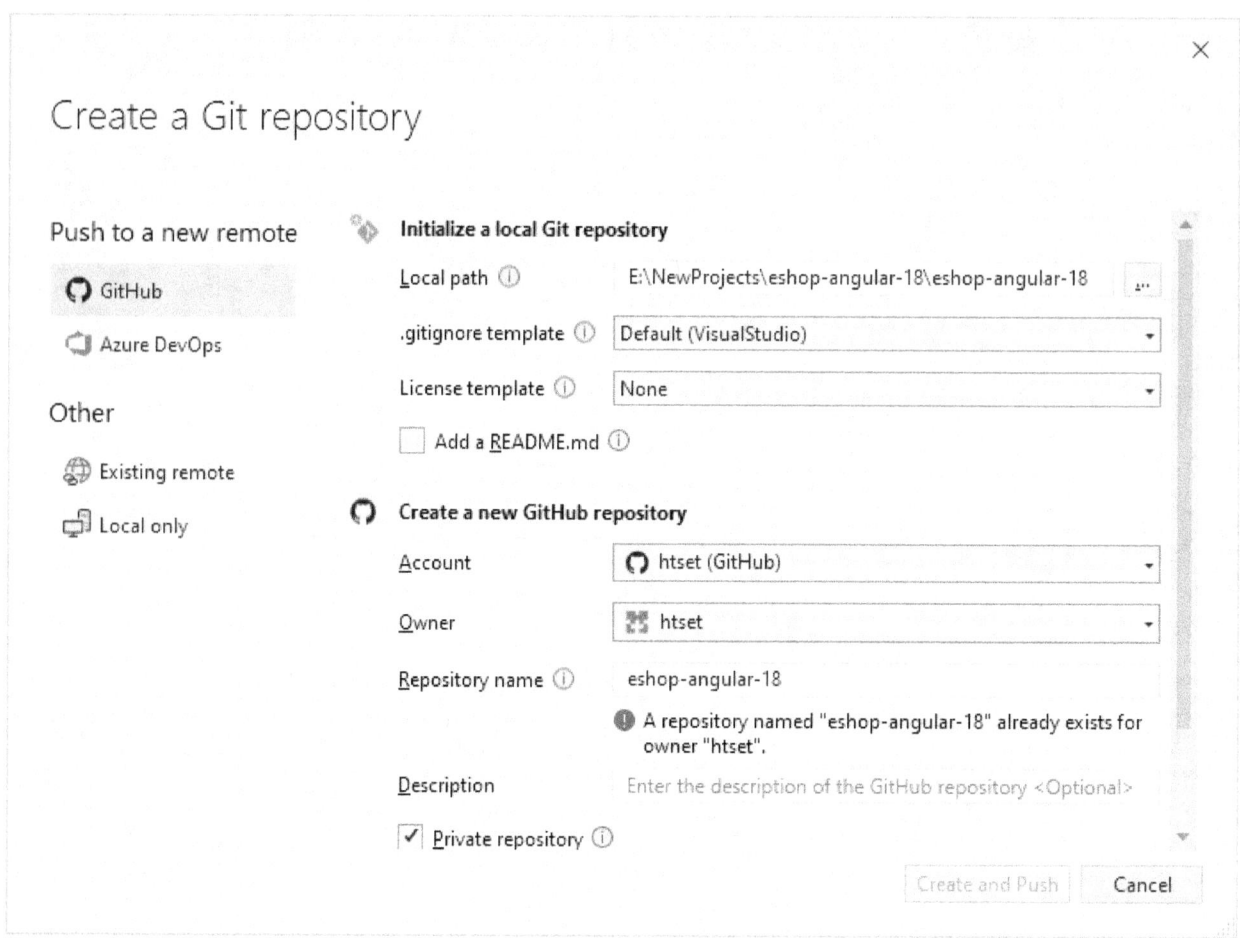

At the beginning of each chapter, we will create a new git branch (e.g. part2 for chapter 2) where we will create all the new code:

git branch part2

git checkout part2

Or, in one command:

git checkout -b part2

At the end of each chapter, we will be merging the respective branch back into the main trunk of the repository:

git merge part2

If you want to test the code at each chapter, you may checkout the respective branch and open it in the IDE. For example, the following command:

git checkout part2

will checkout the code that will have been created by the end of chapter 2.

Now, we are ready to create our first components!

2. Product list and details page

In this chapter, we will create the basic views of our store: the product list and the product details page that will be accessed by customers.

At first, we will use a dummy Angular service to populate both pages. In later iterations of our work, we will introduce data loading from the real API, built with ASP.NET Core.

Data service

In order to leverage some of the advantages that Typescript brings to web programming, we will introduce typing into the project. For start, we create an interface to describe the item structure:

```
export interface Item {
  id: number;
  name: string;
  price: number;
  category: string;
  description?: string;
}
```

LISTING 2-1: item.ts

The '?' operator in the description parameter means that it is optional and can be left undefined in an *Item* object.

Next, we open either a terminal inside Visual Studio or a plain Command Prompt window, and we switch to the frontend project folder. We will create the supporting service (`ItemService`) by issuing the following command:

```
ng generate service Item
```

This service provides two functions:

- To get the list of all available items
- To get one item only (identified by ID)

Both functions return an `Observable`. The components that will eventually call those two functions, will have to subscribe to the returned Observables, in order to get their returned items.

```
import { Injectable, } from '@angular/core';
import { Observable, of } from 'rxjs';
import { Item } from './item';

const mock_items = [
  {
    id: 1, name: 'Adidas Stan Smith', price: 90.0,
    category: 'Shoes', description: ''
```

```
  },
  {
    id: 2, name: 'Nike Air Max', price: 110.0,
    category: 'Shoes', description: ''
  },
  {
    id: 3, name: 'Reebok Sweat Shirt', price: 45.0,
    category: 'Clothes', description: ''
  },
  {
    id: 4, name: 'Puma T-Shirt', price: 30.0,
    category: 'Clothes', description: ''
  },
];

@Injectable({
  providedIn: 'root'
})
export class ItemService {

  getItems(): Observable<Item[]> {
    return of(mock_items);
  }

  getItem(id: number): Observable<Item> {
    return of(mock_items[id - 1]);
  }

  constructor() { }
}
```

LISTING 2-2: item.service.ts

Also note that the service defines an array of dummy products that will be used for testing the components.

Product list component

Our first component provides the listing of all available products; this is where all the items for sale are displayed. For the time being, this list will present the full list of available items. In next versions, we will introduce features like product filtering and pagination.

Before all, we should install *ng-bootstrap*, an Angular library based on Bootstrap that will provide formatting options and a lot of useful components for our web app. For Angular 18, Bootstrap 5 is used.

```
ng add @ng-bootstrap/ng-bootstrap
```

Now, to generate the component:

```
ng generate component Items
```

In the new component's template file, an *ngFor iteration displays the available items in a list:

```html
<p>Products</p>
<div class="row">
  <div *ngFor="let item of items;" class="col-sm-3">
    <div class="card">
      <div class="card-body">
        <h5 class="card-title">
          <a routerLink="/items/{{item.id}}">{{item.name}}</a>
        </h5>
        <p class="card-subtitle mb-2 text-muted">${{item.price}}</p>
      </div>
    </div>
  </div>
</div>
```
LISTING 2-3: items.component.html

Here, we call the getItems function upon initialization and we subscribe to the returned Observable. When the array of items is available, we set the items property, that is used by the component template in the *ngFor loop.

```typescript
import { Component, OnInit } from '@angular/core';
import { ItemService } from '../item.service';
import { Item } from '../item';

@Component({
  selector: 'app-items',
  templateUrl: './items.component.html',
  styleUrl: './items.component.css'
})
export class ItemsComponent implements OnInit {

  items: Item[] = [];

  constructor(private itemService: ItemService) { }

  ngOnInit(): void {
    this.getItems();
  }

  getItems(): void {
    this.itemService.getItems()
      .subscribe(items => {
        this.items = items;
      });
  }
}
```

LISTING 2-4: items.component.ts

We add the following router entries inside the *app-routing.module.ts* file, so that the default route and the /items route will both be handled by `ItemsComponent`.

```
const routes: Routes = [
  {path: '', component: ItemsComponent },
  {path: 'items', component: ItemsComponent }
];
```

LISTING 2-5: app-routing.module.ts

Finally, you may delete the predefined HTML code in *app.component.html* and leave only the <router-outlet> tag at the end of the file. The router outlet is the place where the other components will appear, inside the main page.

```
<router-outlet></router-outlet>
```

Congratulations! You have created you first Angular component. You may give it a try by pressing F5 (debug).

Product details

There are two basic options for the display of the product details, when the user clicks on one of the items in the list:

- Display the details in the same page as the list (in a master-detail kind of view) or,
- Route the user to a new page and display the details there.

The second option is more appropriate to the kind of application we are building here. For instance, now the user will be able to bookmark the selected item and open it later for viewing.

We generate the item details component:

```
ng generate component ItemDetails
```

The ItemDetailsComponent class can have the following form:

```
import { Component, OnInit } from '@angular/core';
import { ActivatedRoute } from '@angular/router';
import { ItemService } from '../item.service';
import { Item } from '../item';

@Component({
  selector: 'app-item-details',
  templateUrl: './item-details.component.html',
  styleUrl: './item-details.component.css'
})
export class ItemDetailsComponent implements OnInit {
```

```
  item:Item = { id: 0, name: "", price: 0, category: "", description: "" };

  constructor(
    private route: ActivatedRoute,
    private itemService: ItemService
  ) { }

  ngOnInit(): void {
    this.getItem();
  }

  getItem(): void {
    const id = Number(this.route.snapshot.paramMap.get('id'));
    if (!isNaN(id)) {
      this.itemService.getItem(id)
        .subscribe((item) => {
          this.item = item;
        })
    }
  }
  addToCart(): void { }
}
```

LISTING 2-6: item-details.component.ts

On initialization, we call the `getItem` function of the Item service, while supplying the selected item ID. The ID is conveyed in the URL (e.g. /items/2) and is accessed using a snapshot of the route:

`const id = Number(this.route.snapshot.paramMap.get('id'));`

We should check for the correctness of the ID and the availability of the item; we will do this in later versions.

Also note that we have to initialize the `item` member variable with a dummy value, so that the component template has something to show until the Observable from `getItem` is resolved and updates `item` with the real value.

The template file is more or less straightforward:

```
<h3>{{item.name}}</h3>
<div>
  <div class="row">
    <div class="col-md-3"><img src="angular.svg" width="200px"></div>
  </div>
  <div class="row">
    <div class="col-md-3">Description: {{item.description}}</div>
  </div>
  <div class="row">
    <div class="col-md-3">Category: {{item.category}}</div>
  </div>
  <div class="row">
```

```
    <div class="col-md-3">Price: {{item.price}}</div>
  </div>
  <div class="row">
    <div class="col-md-3">
      <button (click)="addToCart()" id="addToCart">Add to Cart</button>
    </div>
  </div>
</div>
```

LISTING 2-7: item-details.component.html

Finally, let's not forget to update our routing and we are ready to go!

```
const routes: Routes = [
  {path: '', component: ItemsComponent },
  {path: 'items', component: ItemsComponent },
  {path: 'items/:id', component: ItemDetailsComponent }
];
```

LISTING 2-8: app-routing.module.ts

The code repository for this project is available in GitHub:

https://github.com/htset/eshop-angular-18/tree/part2

3. Pagination

Before creating more components and services, it would be advisable to add some structure to the project. We will create dedicated folders for components, services and models. Furthermore, we will add another level inside the components folder, to differentiate between admin and public components, as well as utility components that are shared.

The new project structure is:

```
-components
    -public
    -admin
    -shared
-services
-models
```

It seems that when we move folders in the Solution Explorer of VS 2022, the imports are not updated to reflect the new folder structure (VS Code does this automatically). Therefore, we will have to update them ourselves. For example, in *item-details.component.ts*, we make the following changes:

```
import { ItemService } from '../../../services/item.service';
import { Item } from '../../../models/item';
```

LISTING 3-1: item-details.component.ts

Since there may be thousands of products in the online shop catalog, the items should be retrieved from the API in batches and not all in one go. Every time the user changes page, a new set of items will be retrieved and displayed in the catalog.

The user will also have the option to change the size of the page, i.e. the number of products displayed at the same time. Here too, a change in the page size will result in the retrieval of the appropriate number of items (and a return to the first page).

For this project, the pagination component from Bootstrap will be used (already installed in the second chapter). First of all, a new interface that describes the payload transported from the API is introduced:

```
import { Item } from "./item";

export interface ItemPayload {
  items: Item[];
  count: number;
}
```

LISTING 3-2: itemPayload.ts

Parameter count contains the *total* number of items contained in the database and will be used to calculate the number of pages. Parameter items contains only the list of items returned after each API call.

Now, we change the dummy ItemService in order to use ItemPayload objects to provide a subset of Items to the component:

```
getItems(page:number, pageSize:number): Observable<ItemPayload> {
  let payload:ItemPayload = {
    items: mock_items.slice((page-1)*pageSize, page*pageSize),
    count: mock_items.length
  }
  return of(payload);
}
```

LISTING 3-3: item.service.ts

In the ItemsComponent template, we add the pagination component, as well as a drop-down control for the selection of page size:

```html
<p>Products</p>

Page size:
<select [(ngModel)]="storeService.pageSize" id="pageSize">
  <option value="3">3</option>
  <option value="5">5</option>
  <option value="10">10</option>
  <option value="50">50</option>
</select>
<br />

<div class="row">
  <div *ngFor="let item of storeService.items;" class="col-sm-3">
    <div class="card" style="width: 15rem">
      <div class="card-body">
        <h5 class="card-title">
          <a routerLink="/items/{{item.id}}">{{item.name}}</a>
        </h5>
        <p class="card-subtitle mb-2 text-muted">${{item.price}}</p>
      </div>
    </div>
  </div>
</div>

<ngb-pagination [(page)]="storeService.page"
                [pageSize]="storeService.pageSize"
                [collectionSize]="storeService.count"
                (pageChange)="onPageChange($event)">
</ngb-pagination>
```

LISTING 3-4: items.component.html

The ngb-pagination component takes the following parameters:

- page: the current page
- pageSize: the selected page size
- collectionSize: the total count of the items
- pageChange: the handler for the page changing event

We need to store the first three parameters in centralized storage so that they will remain available when we leave the catalog page (e.g. to view the details of a product) and then return back to it.

If those variables were stored locally in the component, we would always return to the first page of the catalog and this page would have again the default page size.

For this reason, we will introduce state management functionality in the project. As the web application grows in size and complexity, our life will be easier if we keep state, especially data that is shared between components, in a central store.

There are different approaches with regard to store management. For this project we will follow the simple solution of an Angular service that uses RxJS BehaviorSubject objects to store data and make them available to components.

Another popular option would the NgRx state management library that is based on the Flux/Redux concepts. However, NgRx is a bit complicated and would be more appropriate for large scale projects.

The basic idea behind this approach is to store each shared variable inside its own `BehaviorSubject` object:

```
import { Injectable } from '@angular/core';
import { BehaviorSubject } from 'rxjs';

@Injectable({
  providedIn: 'root'
})
export class StoreService {

  private readonly _items = new BehaviorSubject<Item[]>([]);
  readonly items$ = this._items.asObservable();

  get items(): Item[] {
    return this._items.getValue();
  }

  set items(val: Item[]) {
    this._items.next(val);
  }

  private readonly _page = new BehaviorSubject<number>(1);
  readonly page$ = this._page.asObservable();

  get page(): number {
    return this._page.getValue();
  }
```

```
  set page(val: number) {
    this._page.next(val);
  }

  private readonly _pageSize = new BehaviorSubject<number>(3);
  public pageSize$ = this._pageSize.asObservable();

  get pageSize(): number {
    return this._pageSize.getValue();
  }

  set pageSize(val: number) {
    this._pageSize.next(val);
  }

  private readonly _count = new BehaviorSubject<number>(1);
  readonly count$ = this._count.asObservable();

  get count(): number {
    return this._count.getValue();
  }

  set count(val: number) {
    this._count.next(val);
  }

  constructor() { }
}
```

LISTING 3-5: store.service.ts

By using the `next()` method of the BehaviorSubject object we can update the value that is stored in it. Moreover, by subscribing to the `page$` or `pageSize$` Observable, a component can be notified about any change in this value.

Also, the `ItemsComponent` class now looks like this:

```
import { Component, OnInit } from '@angular/core';
import { ItemService } from '../../../services/item.service';
import { Item } from '../../../models/item';
import { StoreService } from '../../../services/store.service';

@Component({
  selector: 'app-items',
  templateUrl: './items.component.html',
  styleUrl: './items.component.css'
})
export class ItemsComponent implements OnInit {

  constructor(
    private itemService: ItemService,
    public storeService: StoreService) { }
```

```
  ngOnInit(): void {
    this.storeService.pageSizeChanges$
      .subscribe(newPageSize => {
        this.storeService.page = 1;
        this.getItems();
      });

    this.getItems();
  }

  getItems(): void {
    this.itemService.getItems(this.storeService.page,
      this.storeService.pageSize)
      .subscribe(itemPayload => {
        this.storeService.items = itemPayload.items;
        this.storeService.count = itemPayload.count;
      });
  }
}
```

LISTING 3-6: items.component.ts

Note that we need to add `FormsModule` in the `imports` list in *app.module.ts* file, in order to have `ngModel` directive available in the app module. If we forget it, we will get an error like this one:

`error NG8002: Can't bind to 'ngModel' since it isn't a known property of 'select'.`

The last snippet shows, among others, the use of the `pageSize$` observable. More specifically, we subscribe to this `BehaviorSubject` in order to get notified of any changes in the size of the page.

After playing with the web app, changing pages and viewing products, it seems that pagination does not operate as expected. For example, when the user moves to page 2, views a product and returns to the main page catalog, then the catalog moves to page 1 (and does not remain in page 2 as intended).

The reason lies on the nature of BehaviorSubject: When we subscribe to observable `pageSize$` in `ngOnInit` method, the value stored in the respective BehaviorSubject object is immediately emitted. This results in resetting page variable to 1 as can been seen in the previous snippet.

The solution to this problem is the use of a plain RxJS `Subject` object to store the page size value. `Subject` does not return the current value when being subscribed to and triggers only when function `next` is called.

StoreService looks like this now:

```
import { Injectable } from '@angular/core';
import { BehaviorSubject, Subject } from 'rxjs';
```

```typescript
import { Item } from '../models/item';

@Injectable({
  providedIn: 'root'
})
export class StoreService {

  private readonly _items = new BehaviorSubject<Item[]>([]);
  readonly items$ = this._items.asObservable();

  get items(): Item[] {
    return this._items.getValue();
  }

  set items(val: Item[]) {
    this._items.next(val);
  }

  private readonly _page = new BehaviorSubject<number>(1);
  readonly page$ = this._page.asObservable();

  get page(): number {
    return this._page.getValue();
  }

  set page(val: number) {
    this._page.next(val);
  }

  public pageSize: number = 3;
  public readonly _pageSizeSubject = new Subject<number>();
  public pageSizeChanges$ = this._pageSizeSubject.asObservable();

  private readonly _count = new BehaviorSubject<number>(1);
  readonly count$ = this._count.asObservable();

  get count(): number {
    return this._count.getValue();
  }

  set count(val: number) {
    this._count.next(val);
  }

  constructor() { }
}
```

LISTING 3-7: store.service.ts

The items template has also a modified <select> element:

```
<select [(ngModel)]="storeService.pageSize"
    (change)="onPageSizeChange()" id="pageSize">
```

```html
    <option value="3">3</option>
    <option value="5">5</option>
    <option value="10">10</option>
    <option value="50">50</option>
</select>
```

LISTING 3-8: items.component.ts

Also, we modify the ItemsComponent class like this:

```typescript
import { Component, OnInit } from '@angular/core';
import { ItemService } from '../../../services/item.service';
import { Item } from '../../../models/item';
import { StoreService } from '../../../services/store.service';

@Component({
  selector: 'app-items',
  templateUrl: './items.component.html',
  styleUrl: './items.component.css'
})
export class ItemsComponent implements OnInit {

  constructor(
    private itemService: ItemService,
    public storeService: StoreService) { }

  ngOnInit(): void {
    this.storeService.pageSizeChanges$
      .subscribe(newPageSize => {
        this.storeService.page = 1;
        this.getItems();
      });

    this.getItems();
  }

  getItems(): void {
    this.itemService.getItems(this.storeService.page,
      this.storeService.pageSize)
      .subscribe(itemPayload => {
        this.storeService.items = itemPayload.items;
        this.storeService.count = itemPayload.count;
      });
  }

  onPageChange(newPage: number): void {
    this.storeService.page = newPage;
    this.getItems();
  }

  onPageSizeChange(): void {
    this.storeService._pageSizeSubject.next(this.storeService.pageSize);
  }
```

}

LISTING 3-9: **items.component.ts**

In the above, a handler function (`onPageSizeChange()`) has been added to push the newly selected page size value to the Subject.

The code repository of this part is available in GitHub:

https://github.com/htset/eshop-angular-18/tree/part3

4. Product filtering

In this chapter, we will create a filtering component for the product catalog page. We start by generating the component that implements filtering functionality. This component will be placed in the components/shared folder, as it may be used also in other places.

The FilterComponent class has the following form:

```
import { Component, OnInit } from '@angular/core';
import { Filter } from '../../../models/filter';
import { StoreService } from '../../../services/store.service';
import { NgbActiveModal } from '@ng-bootstrap/ng-bootstrap';

@Component({
  selector: 'app-filter',
  templateUrl: './filter.component.html',
  styleUrls: ['./filter.component.css']
})
export class FilterComponent implements OnInit {
  categories = [
    { name: "Shoes", selected: false },
    { name: "Clothes", selected: false },
    { name: "Gear", selected: false }
  ];

  tempFilter: Filter = { name: "", categories: [] };

  constructor(
    public storeService: StoreService,
    public activeModal: NgbActiveModal
  ) { }

  ngOnInit(): void {
    this.tempFilter = this.storeService.filter;
    this.categories = this.categories
      .map(cat =>
      ({
        name: cat.name,
        selected: (this.tempFilter.categories.includes(cat.name))
      }));
  }

  onChange(): void {
    this.tempFilter.categories = this.categories
      .filter(c => c.selected)
      .map(cc => cc.name);
  }

  onFilterChanged(): void {
    this.storeService.filter = this.tempFilter;
  }
}
```

LISTING 4-1: filter.component.ts

This class uses the definition of Filter interface:

```
export interface Filter{
    name: string;
    categories:string[];
}
```

LISTING 4-2: filter.ts

Also, the actively used filter is stored centrally inside StoreService:

```
...
private    readonly    _filter    =    new    BehaviorSubject<Filter>({name:    "",
categories:[]});
readonly filter$ = this._filter.asObservable();

get filter(): Filter {
  return this._filter.getValue();
}

set filter(val: Filter) {
  this._filter.next(val);
}
...
```

LISTING 4-3: store.service.ts

Finally, the template file for the FilterComponent class is depicted below:

```html
<div class="modal-header">
  <h4 class="modal-title">Products Filtering</h4>
  <button type="button" class="close"
          (click)="activeModal.dismiss()">x</button>
</div>

<div class="modal-body">
  <strong>By text:</strong>
  <input type="text" #searchBox id="searchbox"
    [(ngModel)]="tempFilter.name" /><br />
  <strong>By category:</strong>
  <ul>
    <li *ngFor="let cat of categories" style="list-style-type:none;">
      <input type="checkbox" [(ngModel)]="cat.selected"
             id={{cat.name}} (change)="onChange()" />
      {{cat.name}}
    </li>
  </ul>
</div>
```

```html
<div class="modal-footer">
  <button type="button" id="update" class="btn btn-outline-dark"
          (click)="onFilterChanged()">Update Filter</button>
  <button type="button" class="btn btn-outline-dark"
          (click)="activeModal.close()">Close</button>
</div>
```

LISTING 4-4: filter.component.html

The filter component will appear in a modal window when the user clicks on the *filters* button in the product list. For this reason, `FilterComponent` injects ng-bootstrap's `NgbActiveModal` class, in order to be able to `close()` or `dismiss()` the modal window from within.

The modal window will be opened from a button in the product catalog:

```html
<button (click)="openFilter()">Filters</button>
```

LISTING 4-5: items.component.html

The ItemsComponent class will now have the following form:

```typescript
import { Component, OnInit } from '@angular/core';
import { ItemService } from '../../../services/item.service';
import { StoreService } from '../../../services/store.service';
import { NgbModal } from '@ng-bootstrap/ng-bootstrap';
import { skip } from 'rxjs';
import { FilterComponent } from '../../shared/filter/filter.component';

@Component({
  selector: 'app-items',
  templateUrl: './items.component.html',
  styleUrl: './items.component.css'
})
export class ItemsComponent implements OnInit {

  constructor(
    private itemService: ItemService,
    public storeService: StoreService,
    private modalService: NgbModal) { }

  ngOnInit(): void {
    this.storeService.pageSizeChanges$
      .subscribe(newPageSize => {
        this.storeService.page = 1;
        this.getItems();
      });

    this.storeService.filter$
      .pipe(skip(1))    //skip getting filter at component creation
      .subscribe(filter => {
```

```
      this.storeService.page = 1;
      this.getItems();
    });

  this.getItems();
}

getItems(): void {
  this.itemService.getItems(this.storeService.page,
    this.storeService.pageSize,
    this.storeService.filter)
    .subscribe(itemPayload => {
      this.storeService.items = itemPayload.items;
      this.storeService.count = itemPayload.count;
    });
}

onPageChange(newPage: number): void {
  this.storeService.page = newPage;
  this.getItems();
}

onPageSizeChange(): void {
  this.storeService._pageSizeSubject.next(this.storeService.pageSize);
}

openFilter(): void {
  this.modalService.open(FilterComponent);
}
}
```

LISTING 4-6: items.component.ts

ItemsComponent injects ng-bootstrap's ModalService to be able to open a modal window inside the product catalog. Furthermore, the component subscribes to the filter$ Observable from StoreService, so that it will be notified of any change in the filter contents by the user. Note that the component skips getting the filter on the first time it loads to avoid returning to the first page.

Finally, ItemService is updated to provide for the filtering of the (still dummy) items:

```
import { Injectable, } from '@angular/core';
import { Observable, of } from 'rxjs';
import { Item } from '../models/item';
import { ItemPayload } from '../models/itemPayload';
import { Filter } from '../models/filter';

const mock_items: ItemPayload = {
  items: [
    {
      id: 1, name: 'Adidas Stan Smith',
      price: 90.0, category: 'Shoes', description: ''
```

```typescript
    },
    {
      id: 2, name: 'Nike Air Max',
      price: 110.0, category: 'Shoes', description: ''
    },
    {
      id: 3, name: 'Reebok Sweat Shirt',
      price: 45.0, category: 'Clothes', description: ''
    },
    {
      id: 4, name: 'Puma T-Shirt',
      price: 30.0, category: 'Clothes', description: ''
    },
    {
      id: 5, name: 'Under Armour',
      price: 130.0, category: 'Shoes', description: ''
    },
    {
      id: 6, name: 'Nike Sweat shirt',
      price: 65.0, category: 'Clothes', description: ''
    },
    {
      id: 7, name: 'Spalding basketball',
      price: 43.0, category: 'Gear', description: ''
    },
    {
      id: 8, name: 'Dumbbell 5kg',
      price: 3.50, category: 'Gear', description: ''
    },
    {
      id: 9, name: 'New Balance',
      price: 120.0, category: 'Shoes', description: ''
    }
  ],
  count: 8
};

@Injectable({
  providedIn: 'root'
})
export class ItemService {

  getItems(page: number, pageSize: number, filter: Filter):
    Observable<ItemPayload> {
    let filteredItems: Item[] = mock_items.items.filter(item => {
      return (
        item.name.indexOf(filter.name) >= 0
        &&
        (filter.categories.length == 0
          || filter.categories.includes(item.category))
      );
    }
    );

    let payload: ItemPayload = {
```

```
    items: filteredItems.slice((page - 1) * pageSize, page * pageSize),
    count: filteredItems.length
  }
  return of(payload);
}

getItem(id: number): Observable<Item> {
  return of(mock_items.items[id - 1]);
}

constructor() { }
}
```

LISTING 4-7: item.service.ts

The code repository of this chapter is available in GitHub:

https://github.com/htset/eshop-angular-18/tree/part4

5. Cart functionality

On this chapter of the online shop tutorial, we will create the Cart component. We start by defining the types for the cart and the items it contains.

The structure of the cart items is defined in models/cartItem.ts:

```typescript
import { Item } from "./item";

export class CartItem {
  public item: Item = {
    id: 0, name: "", price: 0,
    category: "", description: ""
  };
  public quantity: number = 0;
}
```

LISTING 5-1: cartItem.ts

Next, models/cart.ts implements the functionality of the cart. Note that when the user adds to the cart, a product that is already there, its quantity is increased accordingly.

```typescript
import { CartItem } from "./cartItem";

export class Cart {
  cartItems: CartItem[] = [];

  addItem(cartItem: CartItem) {
    let found: boolean = false;
    this.cartItems = this.cartItems.map(ci => {
      if (ci.item?.id == cartItem.item?.id) {
        ci.quantity++;
        found = true;
      }
      return ci;
    });

    if (!found) {
      this.cartItems.push(cartItem);
    }
  }

  removeItem(item: CartItem) {
    const index = this.cartItems.indexOf(item, 0);
    if (index > -1) {
      this.cartItems.splice(index, 1);
    }
  }

  emptyCart() {
    this.cartItems = [];
  }
```

```
  getTotalValue(): number {
    let sum = this.cartItems.reduce(
      (a, b) => { a = a + b.item?.price * b.quantity; return a; }, 0);
    return sum;
  }

  isCartValid(): boolean {
    if (this.cartItems
      .find(cartitem =>
        (cartitem.quantity == null || cartitem.quantity <= 0)) === undefined)
      return true;
    return false;
  }
}
```

LISTING 5-2: cart.ts

Next, we proceed with generating the cart component:

`ng generate component cart`

This component will depict a list of all products included in the cart, along with their quantities and prices. The user will be able to change the quantity of an item or remove it altogether from the cart. The cart will also present the total amount for payment, as well as options to empty the cart or proceed to checkout.

The cart component template has the following form:

```
<h3>Cart Details</h3>
<table class="table table-striped">
  <tr>
    <th> </th>
    <th>Name</th>
    <th>Unit Price</th>
    <th>Quantity</th>
    <th>Total Price</th>
    <th> </th>
  </tr>
  <tr *ngFor="let item of storeService.cart.cartItems">
    <td>
      <a routerLink="/items/{{item.item.id}}">
        <img src="angular.svg" width="70px" />
      </a>
    </td>
    <td>
      <a routerLink="/items/{{item.item.id}}">
        {{item.item.name}}
      </a>
    </td>
    <td>
      <a routerLink="/items/{{item.item.id}}">
        {{item.item.price}}
```

```html
      </a>
    </td>
    <td>
      <input type="number" [(ngModel)]="item.quantity"
             size="2" id="quantity" />
    </td>
    <td>
      <a routerLink="/items/{{item.item.id}}">
        {{item.item.price * item.quantity}}
      </a>
    </td>
    <td>
      <input type="button" (click)="removeFromCart(item)"
             id="remove" value="Remove" />
    </td>
  </tr>
  <tr>
    <td colspan="4"> </td>
    <td>{{storeService.cart.getTotalValue()}}</td>
    <td> </td>
  </tr>
</table>
<br />
<br />
<button (click)="emptyCart()" id="empty"
        [disabled]="storeService.cart.cartItems.length == 0">
  Empty Cart
</button>
<br />
<br />
<button routerLink="/checkout" id="checkout"
        [disabled]="storeService.cart.cartItems.length == 0
            || !storeService.cart.isCartValid()">
  Go to Checkout..
</button>
<br />
<br />
<button routerLink="">Back to items</button>
<br />
```

LISTING 5-3: cart.component.html

The CartComponent class contains functions for removing one or all items from the cart:

```typescript
import { Component, OnInit } from "@angular/core";
import { CartItem } from "../../../models/cartItem";
import { StoreService } from "../../../services/store.service";

@Component({
  selector: 'app-cart',
  templateUrl: './cart.component.html',
  styleUrls: ['./cart.component.css']
})
```

```typescript
export class CartComponent implements OnInit {

  constructor(public storeService: StoreService) { }

  removeFromCart(item: CartItem){
    this.storeService.cart.removeItem(item);
  }

  emptyCart(){
    this.storeService.cart.emptyCart();
  }

  ngOnInit(): void {
  }

}
```

LISTING 5-4: cart.component.ts

The state information about the cart (cart variable) is stored inside StoreService with the use of a BehaviorSubject object:

```typescript
...
  private readonly _cart = new BehaviorSubject<Cart>(new Cart());
  readonly cart$ = this._cart.asObservable();

  get cart(): Cart {
    return this._cart.getValue();
  }

  set cart(val: Cart) {
    this._cart.next(val);
  }
...
```

LISTING 5-5: store.service.ts

Users may add a product in the cart, by pressing the *Add to cart* button in the item details component:

```typescript
...
export class ItemDetailsComponent implements OnInit {

  item:Item = {id:0, name:"", price:0, category:"", description:""};

  constructor(
    private route: ActivatedRoute,
    private itemService: ItemService,
    private storeService: StoreService,
    private router: Router
  ) { }
```

```
...
  addToCart(): void {
    this.storeService.cart.addItem({item: this.item, quantity: 1});
    this.router.navigate(['/cart']);
  }

}
```

LISTING 5-6: item-details.component.ts

In order to be able to navigate to the cart page, the respective route entry should be added in app-routing.module.ts:

```
const routes: Routes = [
  {path: '', component: ItemsComponent },
  {path: 'items', component: ItemsComponent },
  {path: 'items/:id', component: ItemDetailsComponent }  ,
  {path: 'cart', component: CartComponent}
];
```

LISTING 5-7: app-routing.module.ts

Finally, we may add a link to the cart page in `AppComponent` so that users will be able to navigate to the cart from any page:

```
<div *ngIf="storeService.cart.cartItems.length > 0" align="right">
    <a routerLink='cart'>Cart</a>
</div>
<router-outlet></router-outlet>
```

LISTING 5-8: app.component.html

Finally, we should declare `StoreService` in the constructor of the `AppComponent` class:

```
@Component({
  selector: 'app-root',
  templateUrl: './app.component.html',
  styleUrls: ['./app.component.css']
})
export class AppComponent {
  title = 'my-eshop';

  constructor(
    public storeService: StoreService
  ) { }
}
```

LISTING 5-9: app.component.ts

Note that the cart needs more functionality, mainly with regard to error handling and input processing. For instance, the cart component should check that the quantity is an integer and inform the user accordingly. Such issues have been left out for simplicity reasons and will be dealt with in a later chapter, where an overall solution for error handling will be presented.

The code repository of this part is available in GitHub:

https://github.com/htset/eshop-angular-18/tree/part5

6. Creating the ASP.NET Core 8 Web API

So far, our Angular frontend has used a dummy API for displaying products. Now, it is time to use a real API, so we will develop the ASP.NET Core Web API we created on the first chapter of this book.

We will need to use a database to store our data. Any recent version of SQL Server will do just fine, but you can use any other database, like MySQL or MariaDB.

First of all, we proceed with the installation of the Entity Framework (version 8) through the Package Manager Console:

```
PM>Install-Package Microsoft.EntityFrameworkCore.SqlServer
PM>Install-Package Microsoft.EntityFrameworkCore.Tools
```

The latest version (8.0.7) was installed for both packages. Alternatively, we can install the packages from the NuGet package manager in Visual Studio.

Next, structure is added to the project, by creating Models and Services folders.

Models

For this project, the Code-First approach will be followed. This means that the models will first be created in code, i.e. in plain C# classes (POCOs). With the use of the Entity Framework migration tools, the database and the respective tables will be created automatically.

Inside the Models folder, we add the definition of Item and ItemPayload classes that will be used to describe the structure of the Items database table and the structure of the JSON data that will be transmitted to the API client respectively.

```csharp
namespace eshop_angular_18.Server.Models
{
  public class Item
  {
    public int Id { get; set; }
    public string? Name { get; set; }
    public decimal Price { get; set; }
    public string? Category { get; set; }
    public string? Description { get; set; }
  }
}
```

LISTING 6-1: Item.cs

```csharp
namespace eshop_angular_18.Server.Models
{
  public class ItemPayload
```

```
  {
    public List<Item> Items { get; set; }
    public int Count { get; set; }

    public ItemPayload(List<Item> Items, int Count)
    {
      this.Items = Items;
      this.Count = Count;
    }
  }
}
```

LISTING 6-2: ItemPayload.cs

In order to be able to store objects of Item class in the database, we need a context class. The `Items` property inside the `EshopContext` class provides access to the set of `Item` entities in the database:

```
using Microsoft.EntityFrameworkCore;

namespace eshop_angular_18.Server.Models
{
  public class EshopContext : DbContext
  {
    public EshopContext(DbContextOptions<EshopContext> options)
        : base(options)
    {
    }

    public DbSet<Item> Items { get; set; }
  }
}
```

LISTING 6-3: EshopContext.cs

Next, we add a connection string to appsettings.json file:

```
{
  "Logging": {
    "LogLevel": {
      "Default": "Information",
      "Microsoft.AspNetCore": "Warning"
    }
  },
  "AllowedHosts": "*",
  "ConnectionStrings": {
    "DefaultConnection": "Data Source=localhost\\SQLEXPRESS;Initial Catalog=angular-eshop-18-DB;Integrated Security=SSPI; Encrypt=False;"
  }
}
```

LISTING 6-4: appsettings.json

This connection string implies that we will use an SQL Server database, named *angular-eshop-db*. We will connect to the database with Windows Authentication.

The connection string will be used in *Program.cs* file:

```
...
var connectionString =
    builder.Configuration.GetConnectionString("DefaultConnection");
builder.Services.AddDbContext<EshopContext>(x =>
    x.UseSqlServer(connectionString));

var app = builder.Build();
...
```

LISTING 6-5: Program.cs

The final step with regard to models is to apply the first migration on the database. This will result in the creation of the database in the first place, as well as the creation of the Items table, according to the definition of the Item class.

In order to handle migrations, library Microsoft.EntityFrameworkCore.Tools should be installed.

In the Package Manager window, we add the initial migration:

```
PM> Add-Migration InitialCreate
```

The migration will be created, but with the following warning:

```
No store type was specified for the decimal property 'Price' on entity type 'Item'.
This will cause values to be silently truncated if they do not fit in the default
precision and scale. Explicitly specify the SQL server column type that can
accommodate all the values in 'OnModelCreating' using 'HasColumnType', specify
precision and scale using 'HasPrecision', or configure a value converter using
'HasConversion'.
To undo this action, use Remove-Migration.
```

Therefore, we have to remove the existing migration first:

```
PM> Remove-Migration
```

It seems that we have to explicitly define the type of the Price column inside the Item context class. This can be performed by implementing an `OnModelCreating` method inside the `EshopContext` class:

```
using Microsoft.EntityFrameworkCore;

namespace eshop_angular_18.Server.Models
{
  public class EshopContext : DbContext
  {
    public EshopContext(DbContextOptions<EshopContext> options)
        : base(options)
    {
    }

    public DbSet<Item> Items { get; set; }

    protected override void OnModelCreating(ModelBuilder modelBuilder)
    {
      modelBuilder.Entity<Item>().Property(p =>
         p.Price).HasColumnType("decimal(18,2)");
    }
  }
}
```

LISTING 6-6: EshopContext.cs

Now, the migration will be created successfully, and the respective class will appear in the Migrations folder in Solution Explorer. Next, by running:

```
PM> Update-Database
```

in the Package Manager window, the migration is applied to the database. If needed, the migration can be reverted by using the name of the previous one:

```
PM> Update-Database –Migration "target migration name"
```

And then the migration class itself can be removed from the project:

```
PM> Remove-Migration
```

You can run the following script in the SQL Management Studio to add some items in the database:

```
USE [angular-eshop-18-DB]
GO

INSERT INTO [dbo].[Items]
```

```
        ([Name]
        ,[Price]
        ,[Category]
        ,[Description])
    VALUES
        ('Adidas Stan Smith', 90.0, 'Shoes', ''),
        ('Nike Air Max', 110.0, 'Shoes', ''),
        ('Reebok Sweat Shirt', 45.0, 'Clothes', ''),
        ('Puma T-Shirt', 30.0, 'Clothes', ''),
        ('Under Armour', 130.0, 'Shoes', ''),
        ('Nike Sweat shirt', 65.0, 'Clothes', ''),
        ('Spalding basketball', 43.0, 'Gear', ''),
        ('Dumbbell 5kg', 3.50, 'Gear', ''),
        ('New Balance', 120.0, 'Shoes', '')
GO
```

LISTING 6-7: SQL command

Controller

Now, the Items controller class will be added to the project. For the time being, it will serve only requests for one (e.g. GET /api/items/5) or all items (GET /api/items) in the database.

We choose to create an Empty API Controller:

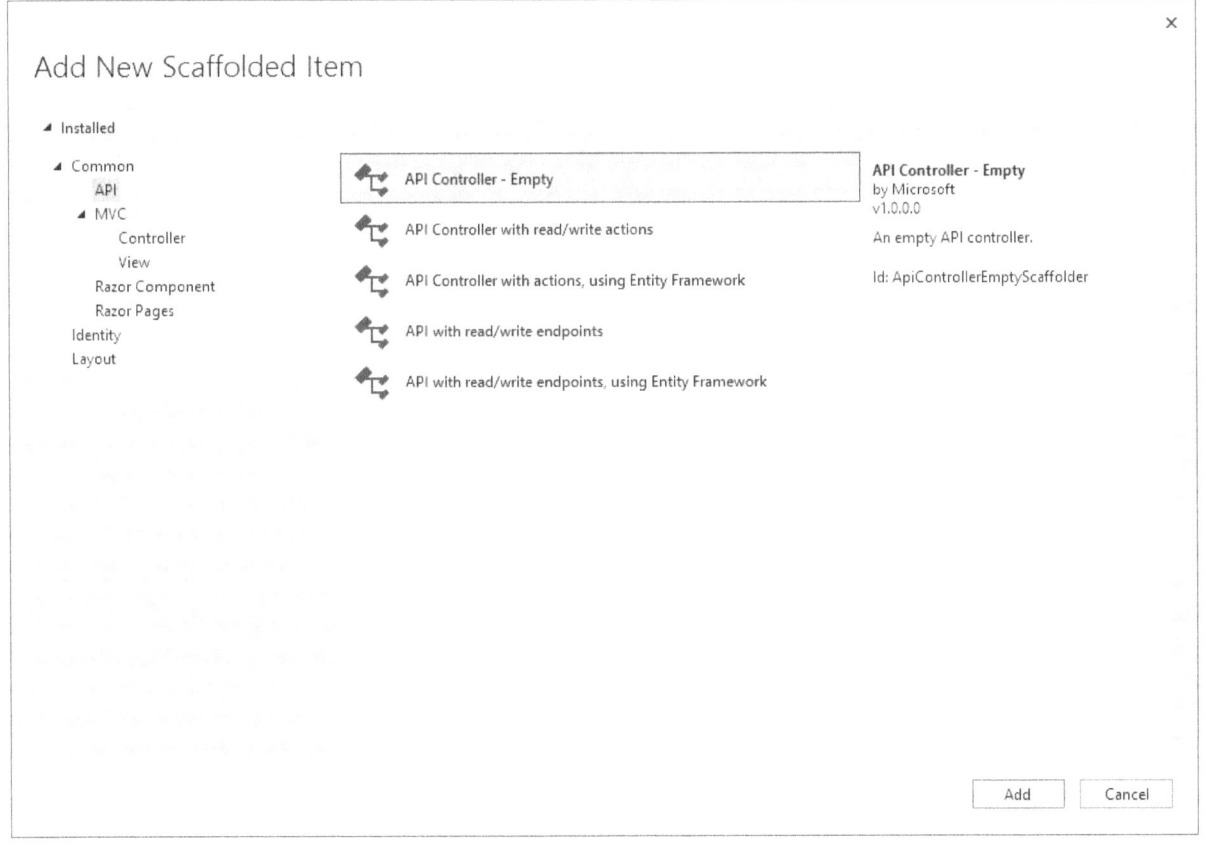

The Items controller has the following form:

```csharp
using eshop_angular_18.Server.Models;
using Microsoft.AspNetCore.Mvc;
using Microsoft.EntityFrameworkCore;

namespace eshop_angular_18.Server.Controllers
{
  [Route("api/items")]
  [ApiController]
  public class ItemController : ControllerBase
  {
    private readonly EshopContext _context;

    public ItemController(EshopContext context)
    {
      _context = context;
    }

    [HttpGet]
    public async Task<ActionResult<ItemPayload>> GetItems()
    {
      int count = await _context.Items.CountAsync();
      List<Item> list = await _context.Items.ToListAsync();
      return new ItemPayload(list, count);
    }

    [HttpGet("{id}")]
    public async Task<ActionResult<Item>> GetItem(int id)
    {
      var Item = await _context.Items.FindAsync(id);
      if (Item == null)
      {
        return NotFound();
      }
      return Item;
    }
  }
}
```

LISTING 6-8: ItemController.cs

This is a very simple implementation of the controller as there are no options for pagination, filtering and sorting that would be necessary to our frontend. In the next chapter, this functionality will be included in the controller and the API will be made available to the Angular frontend.

Now we can run the solution by pressing F5 (Start). As before, the default browser will open pointing to the frontend address (`https://localhost:4200`). To see the backend and get the list of all items that we inserted in the database, we should go to:

`https://localhost:7141/api/items`

Note that this port may be different on your machine, so you will have to check it in *appsettings.json* file.

To get the item with ID=1, we should use the following URL:
`https://localhost:7141/api/items/1`

You can also use the Swagger UI to access your new API at:
`https://localhost:7141/swagger/index.html`

The resulting project can be found in Github:

https://github.com/htset/eshop-angular-18/tree/part6

7. API pagination and frontend-backend integration

In this chapter we will continue developing the ASP.NET Core Web API by introducing pagination and integration with the Angular frontend.

API Pagination

The API, as it stands now, needs pagination so that a request to /api/items will not return the whole inventory of products. The API will have options, not only for pagination, but also for product filtering, based on the name and the category of the product. The get request to /api/items will have the following format:

/api/items?pageNumber=1&pageSize=10&name=Adidas&category=shoes#clothes

In particular, the category parameter will have all requested categories concatenated with the use of the hash (#) symbol.

Let's start with the `ItemController` class and modify the `GetItems` method, so that it can process the query string and filter the products based on the user's request:

```
...
[HttpGet]
public async Task<ActionResult<ItemPayload>> GetItems(
        [FromQuery] QueryStringParameters qsParameters)
{
  IQueryable<Item> returnItems = _context.Items.OrderBy(on => on.Id);

  if (qsParameters.Name != null
          && !qsParameters.Name.Trim().Equals(string.Empty))
      returnItems = returnItems
              .Where(item =>
                      item.Name.ToLower()
                      .Contains(qsParameters.Name.Trim().ToLower()));

  if (qsParameters.Category != null
          && !qsParameters.Category.Trim().Equals(string.Empty))
  {
      string[] categories = qsParameters.Category.Split('#');
      returnItems = returnItems
              .Where(item => categories.Contains(item.Category));
  }

  //get total count before paging
  int count = await returnItems.CountAsync();

  returnItems = returnItems
          .Skip((qsParameters.PageNumber - 1) * qsParameters.PageSize)
          .Take(qsParameters.PageSize);

  List<Item> list = await returnItems.ToListAsync();

  return new ItemPayload(list, count);
```

```
}
...
```
LISTING 7-1: ItemController.cs

Method `GetItems` makes use of the `QueryStringParameters` class to automagically encapsulate the query string parameters sent by the user inside an object. This object is then used to:

- Order results based on item ID
- Filter based on name and category
- Select a subset of products according to the requested page number and size

Class `QueryStringParameters` is depicted in the following:

```
namespace eshop_angular_18.Server.Controllers
{
  public class QueryStringParameters
  {
    const int maxPageSize = 50;
    public int PageNumber { get; set; } = 1;
    private int _pageSize = 10;
    public int PageSize
    {
      get { return _pageSize; }
      set { _pageSize = (value > maxPageSize) ? maxPageSize : value; }
    }
    public string? Name { get; set; } = string.Empty;
    public string? Category { get; set; } = string.Empty;
  }
}
```

LISTING 7-2: QueryStringParameters.cs

Now, our controller is ready to process the complex query string listed above.

Integration with frontend

Next, it is time to modify our Angular frontend, so that it can make use of the new API. Both projects will run on the same server (localhost) but on different ports. The frontend runs on port 4200 by default, while the API runs on an arbitrarily selected port (e.g. 7141), that we can change in *launchSettings.json* configuration file.

First of all, since the frontend and the API technically run on different servers, we need to use CORS (Cross-Origin Resource Sharing), so that browsers will allow this communication to take place.

In the ASP.NET Core Web API, we need to add CORS-specific functionality in *Program.cs* file. More specifically, we add a new CORS policy allowing requests coming from https://localhost:4200:

```
var allowSpecificOrigins = "angular_eshop_AllowSpecificOrigins";

...

builder.Services.AddCors(options =>
{
  options.AddPolicy(allowSpecificOrigins,
        builder =>
          builder.WithOrigins("http://localhost:4200", "https://localhost:4200")
        .AllowAnyMethod()
        .AllowAnyHeader()
        .AllowCredentials());
});
...

app.UseCors(allowSpecificOrigins);
```

LISTING 7-3: Program.cs

Here, we have allowed all kinds of methods and headers, but we can be more restrictive and specify only a subset of them to be allowed to access the API.

Furthermore, we add the `EnableCors` annotation on the ItemController definition along with the CORS string that we selected in Program.cs:

```
[Route("api/items")]
[EnableCors("angular_eshop_AllowSpecificOrigins")]
[ApiController]
public class ItemController : ControllerBase
```

LISTING 7-4: ItemController.cs

On the frontend side, we proceed with modifying `ItemService` class, so that it gets products from the API and not from a dummy list:

```
import { Injectable, } from '@angular/core';
import { Observable, catchError, of } from 'rxjs';
import { Item } from '../models/item';
import { ItemPayload } from '../models/itemPayload';
import { Filter } from '../models/filter';
import { HttpClient, HttpHeaders, HttpParams } from '@angular/common/http';
import { environment } from '../../environments/environment';

@Injectable({
  providedIn: 'root'
})
export class ItemService {
```

```typescript
  itemsUrl = `${environment.apiUrl}/items`;

  httpOptions = {
    headers: new HttpHeaders({ 'Content-Type': 'application/json' })
  };

  getItems(page: number, pageSize: number, filter: Filter)
      : Observable<ItemPayload> {
    let categoriesString: string = "";
    filter.categories
      .forEach(cc => categoriesString = categoriesString + cc + "#");
    if (categoriesString.length > 0)
      categoriesString = categoriesString
        .substring(0, categoriesString.length - 1);

    let params = new HttpParams()
      .set("name", filter.name)
      .set("pageNumber", page.toString())
      .set("pageSize", pageSize.toString())
      .set("category", categoriesString);

    return this.http.get<ItemPayload>(this.itemsUrl, { params: params })
      .pipe(
        catchError(this.handleError<ItemPayload>('getItems',
          { items: [], count: 0 }))
      );
  }

  getItem(id: number): Observable<Item> {
    const url = `${this.itemsUrl}/${id}`;
    return this.http.get<Item>(url)
      .pipe(
        catchError(this.handleError<Item>(`getItem/${id}`,
          { id: 0, name: "", price: 0, category: "", description: "" }))
      );
  }

  handleError<T>(operation = 'operation', result?: T) {
    return (error: any): Observable<T> => {
      console.error(error);
      return of(result as T);
    }
  }

  constructor(private http: HttpClient) { }
}
```

LISTING 7-5: item.service.ts

We should also add `HttpClientModule` in the imports section in *app.module.ts*.

Also, we should define the `apiUrl` parameter inside environments.ts:

```
export const environment = {
  production: false,
  apiUrl: 'https://localhost:7141/api'
};
```

LISTING 7-6: environment.development.ts

After Angular 15, we have to create the `environments` folder ourselves, with:

`ng g environments`

from the *src* folder.

Now, the Angular frontend loads the products list and information from the ASP.NET Core Web API.

You can find the code for this chapter in Github:

https://github.com/htset/eshop-angular-18/tree/part7

8. Authentication

In this chapter we will continue with the implementation of user authentication functionality in our Angular web app.

Frontend

On the Angular side, we first create the login component:

```
<div class="col-md-6 offset-md-3 mt-5">
  <div class="card">
    <h4 class="card-header">Log in</h4>
    <div class="card-body">
      <form [formGroup]="loginForm" (ngSubmit)="onSubmit()">
        <div class="form-group">
          <label for="username">Username</label>
          <input type="text"
                 formControlName="username"
                 class="form-control"
                 [ngClass]="{ 'is-invalid': submitted &&
                   loginForm.controls['username'].errors }" />
          <div *ngIf="submitted && loginForm.controls['username'].errors">
            <div *ngIf="loginForm.controls['username'].errors?.['required']">
              Required
            </div>
          </div>
        </div>
        <div class="form-group">
          <label for="password">Password</label>
          <input type="password"
                 formControlName="password"
                 class="form-control"
                 [ngClass]="{ 'is-invalid': submitted &&
                   loginForm.controls['password'].errors }" />
          <div *ngIf="submitted && loginForm.controls['password'].errors">
            <div *ngIf="loginForm.controls['password'].errors?.['required']">
              Required
            </div>
          </div>
        </div>
        <button [disabled]="loading" class="btn btn-primary" id="login">
          <span *ngIf="loading"
                class="spinner-border spinner-border-sm mr-1"></span>
          Log in
        </button>
        <div *ngIf="error"
             class="alert alert-danger mt-3 mb-3">{{error}}</div>
      </form>
    </div>
  </div>
</div>
```

LISTING 8-1: login.component.html

The login form is implemented using Reactive Forms, so be sure to add the corresponding import (`ReactiveFormsModule`) in *app.module.ts*:

```
@NgModule({
...
  imports: [
...
    ReactiveFormsModule
  ],
  providers: [],
  bootstrap: [AppComponent]
})
export class AppModule { }
```

LISTING 8-2: app.module.ts

LoginComponent class defines a `FormGroup` that contains the two input fields (username and password). Those fields will be marked as "required" during validation on form submit.

```
import { Component, OnInit } from '@angular/core';
import { FormBuilder, FormGroup, Validators } from '@angular/forms';
import { ActivatedRoute, Router } from '@angular/router';
import        {           AuthenticationService          }        from
'../../../services/authentication.service';

@Component({
  selector: 'app-login',
  templateUrl: './login.component.html',
  styleUrls: ['./login.component.css']
})
export class LoginComponent implements OnInit {

  loginForm: FormGroup = new FormGroup({});
  loading: boolean = false;
  submitted: boolean = false;
  error: string = '';

  constructor(
    private formBuilder: FormBuilder,
    public authenticationService: AuthenticationService,
    public route: ActivatedRoute,
    public router: Router
  ) { }

  ngOnInit() {
    this.loginForm = this.formBuilder.group({
      username: ['', Validators.required],
      password: ['', Validators.required]
    });
  }
```

```
  onSubmit() {
    this.submitted = true;

    if (this.loginForm.invalid)
      return;

    this.loading = true;
    this.authenticationService.login(
      this.loginForm.controls['username'].value,
      this.loginForm.controls['password'].value
    )
      .subscribe({
        next: () => {
          const returnUrl
            = this.route.snapshot.queryParams['returnUrl'] || '/';
          this.router.navigate([returnUrl]);
        },
        error: error => {
          this.error = error.error.message;
          this.loading = false;
        }
      });
  }
}
```

LISTING 8-3: login.component.ts

We can see that, in onSubmit(), we call the login() method of a new service (AuthenticationService):

```
import { Injectable } from '@angular/core';
import { StoreService } from './store.service';
import { HttpClient } from '@angular/common/http';
import { environment } from '../../environments/environment';
import { map } from 'rxjs';
import { User } from '../models/user';

@Injectable({
  providedIn: 'root'
})
export class AuthenticationService {

  constructor(
    public storeService: StoreService,
    private http: HttpClient
  ) { }

  login(username: string, password: string) {
    return this.http.post<User>(`${environment.apiUrl}/users/authenticate`,
      { username, password })
      .pipe(
        map(user => {
          sessionStorage.setItem('user', JSON.stringify(user));
```

```
        this.storeService.user = user;
        return user;
      })
    );
  }

  logout() {
    sessionStorage.removeItem('user');
    this.storeService.user = null;
  }
}
```

LISTING 8-4: authentication.service.ts

AuthenticationService calls the backend RESTful method (/users/authenticate) which, on success, returns a User object. This object contains all information about the user that is stored in our database. Moreover, it contains a JWT Authentication Token that will be used in all subsequent requests.

The User object is stringified and stored in the sessionStorage, so that it will available upon page reload. It is also stored in the StoreService object, so that will be available to all objects in the application:

```
....
  private readonly _user
    = new BehaviorSubject<User|null>(
        (sessionStorage.getItem('user')===null) ?
          null : JSON.parse(sessionStorage.getItem('user') ?? "")
    );
  readonly user$ = this._user.asObservable();

  get user(): User|null {
    return this._user.getValue();
  }

  set user(val: User|null) {
    this._user.next(val);
  }
....
```

LISTING 8-5: store.service.ts

Note that the BehaviorSubject object can also receive a null value (when there is no user logged in the application).

The User object has the following form:

```
export class User {
    id?: number;
    username?: string;
```

```
    password?: string;
    firstName?: string;
    lastName?: string;
    token?: string;
    role?: string;
    email?: string;
}
```

LISTING 8-6: user.ts

Next, we need to add the routing entry for the Log in component:

```
...
const routes: Routes = [
  {path: '', component: ItemsComponent },
  {path: 'items', component: ItemsComponent },
  {path: 'items/:id', component: ItemDetailsComponent } ,
  {path: 'cart', component: CartComponent},
  {path: 'login', component: LoginComponent},
];
...
```

LISTING 8-7: app-routing.module.ts

Finally, we may add links to log in/log out, as well as current user information on all pages, through AppComponent:

```
@if (!user?.id){
<div align="right">
  <a routerLink='login'>Log in</a>
</div>
}

@if (storeService.cart.cartItems.length > 0){
<div align="right">
  <a routerLink='cart'>Cart</a>
</div>
}

@if (user?.id){
  <div align="right">
    User: {{user?.username}} |
    <a href="#" (click)="logout($event)">Logout</a>
  </div>
}

<router-outlet></router-outlet>
```

LISTING 8-8: app.component.html

Note that we are using the new `@if` directive in the place of `*ngIf`.

```typescript
import { Component } from '@angular/core';
import { StoreService } from './services/store.service';
import { AuthenticationService } from './services/authentication.service';
import { Router } from '@angular/router';
import { User } from './models/user';

@Component({
  selector: 'app-root',
  templateUrl: './app.component.html',
  styleUrls: ['./app.component.css']
})
export class AppComponent {

  user: User | null = null;

  constructor(
    private router: Router,
    public authenticationService: AuthenticationService,
    public storeService: StoreService
  ) {
    this.storeService.user$.subscribe(x => this.user = x);
  }

  logout(e: Event) {
    e.preventDefault();
    this.authenticationService.logout();
    this.router.navigate(['/login']);
  }
}
```

LISTING 8-9: app.component.ts

Backend

On the ASP.NET Core Web API side, we will have to implement the authentication method that our frontend calls during log in. For this purpose, we will first create our model, the `User` class:

```csharp
namespace eshop_angular_18.Server.Models
{
  public class User
  {
    public int Id { get; set; }
    public string? FirstName { get; set; }
    public string? LastName { get; set; }
    public string? Username { get; set; }
    public string? Password { get; set; }
    public string? Token { get; set; }
    public string? Role { get; set; }
```

```csharp
    public string? Email { get; set; }
  }
}
```

LISTING 8-10: User.cs

Next, we add the necessary context (we use the existing `EshopContext`):

```csharp
using Microsoft.EntityFrameworkCore;

namespace eshop_angular_18.Server.Models
{
  public class EshopContext : DbContext
  {
    public EshopContext(DbContextOptions<EshopContext> options)
        : base(options)
    {
    }

    public DbSet<Item> Items { get; set; }
    public DbSet<User> Users { get; set; }

    protected override void OnModelCreating(ModelBuilder modelBuilder)
    {
      modelBuilder.Entity<Item>().Property(p =>
          p.Price).HasColumnType("decimal(18,2)");
    }
  }
}
```

LISTING 8-11: EshopContext.cs

Since we follow the Code-First approach with regard to databases, we can create the Users table with the use of a migration. In the Package Manager Console, we can now type:

```
PM> Add-Migration UsersAdded
```

```
PM> Update-Database
```

In this way, a new migration is created and is applied against the database. As a result, the `Users` table is created.

Next, we will implement a new controller that will handle the authentication process:

```csharp
using eshop_angular_18.Server.Helpers;
using eshop_angular_18.Server.Models;
using Microsoft.AspNetCore.Cors;
using Microsoft.AspNetCore.Mvc;
using Microsoft.IdentityModel.Tokens;
using System.IdentityModel.Tokens.Jwt;
using System.Security.Claims;
using System.Text;
```

```csharp
namespace eshop_angular_18.Server.Controllers
{
  [Route("api/users")]
  [EnableCors("angular_eshop_AllowSpecificOrigins")]
  [ApiController]
  public class UserController : ControllerBase
  {
    private readonly EshopContext Context;
    private readonly string Secret
        = "this is a very long string to be used as secret";

    public UserController(EshopContext context)
    {
      Context = context;
    }

    [HttpPost("authenticate")]
    public IActionResult Authenticate([FromBody] User formParams)
    {
      if (formParams == null || formParams.Password == null)
        return BadRequest(new { message = "Log in failed" });

      var user = Context.Users
          .SingleOrDefault(x => x.Username == formParams.Username);

      if (user == null || user.Password == null)
        return BadRequest(new { message = "Log in failed" });

      if (!PasswordHasher
          .VerifyPassword(formParams.Password, user.Password))
        return BadRequest(new { message = "Log in failed" });

      user.Token = CreateToken(user);
      user.Password = null;

      return Ok(user);
    }

    private string CreateToken(User user)
    {
      var jwtTokenHandler = new JwtSecurityTokenHandler();
      var key = Encoding.ASCII.GetBytes(Secret);
      var identity = new ClaimsIdentity(new Claim[]
      {
        new Claim(ClaimTypes.Role, user.Role);
      });
      var credentials
          = new SigningCredentials(new SymmetricSecurityKey(key),
              SecurityAlgorithms.HmacSha256);

      var tokenDescriptor = new SecurityTokenDescriptor
      {
        Subject = identity,
        Expires = DateTime.Now.AddMinutes(120),
        SigningCredentials = credentials
```

```
        };

        var token = jwtTokenHandler.CreateToken(tokenDescriptor);
        return jwtTokenHandler.WriteToken(token);
      }
    }
}
```

LISTING 8-12: UserController.cs

The `Authenticate()` method first verifies that the user exists and that the supplied password matches the one stored in the database. Upon success, it creates a JWT Authentication Token and returns it to the caller (along with all user information stored in the database).

We use a claims-based authentication scheme, where the user ID is stored inside the token and is used in the backend to identify the user.

The controller makes use of the `PasswordHasher` class and its two static methods:

- a method to create the hash of a password string
- a method to verify that the hash of a supplied password matches the hash stored in the database:

```
using System.Security.Cryptography;

namespace eshop_angular_18.Server.Helpers
{
  public class PasswordHasher
  {
    private static RandomNumberGenerator rng =
        RandomNumberGenerator.Create();
    private static readonly int SaltSize = 16;
    private static readonly int HashSize = 20;
    private static readonly int Iterations = 10000;

    public static string HashPassword(string password)
    {
      byte[] salt;
      rng.GetBytes(salt = new byte[SaltSize]);

      var key = new Rfc2898DeriveBytes(password, salt, Iterations,
          HashAlgorithmName.SHA256);
      var hash = key.GetBytes(HashSize);

      var hashBytes = new byte[SaltSize + HashSize];
      Array.Copy(salt, 0, hashBytes, 0, SaltSize);
      Array.Copy(hash, 0, hashBytes, SaltSize, HashSize);

      var base64Hash = Convert.ToBase64String(hashBytes);
```

```csharp
      return base64Hash;
    }

    public static bool VerifyPassword(string password, string base64Hash)
    {
      var hashBytes = Convert.FromBase64String(base64Hash);

      var salt = new byte[SaltSize];
      Array.Copy(hashBytes, 0, salt, 0, SaltSize);

      var key = new Rfc2898DeriveBytes(password, salt, Iterations,
        HashAlgorithmName.SHA256);
      byte[] hash = key.GetBytes(HashSize);

      for (var i = 0; i < HashSize; i++)
      {
        if (hashBytes[i + SaltSize] != hash[i])
          return false;
      }
      return true;
    }
  }
}
```

LISTING 8-13: **PasswordHasher.cs**

The above solution focuses solely on the authentication of a user, i.e. checking the user's credentials against those stored in a database and sending a JWT Token that will be eventually stored in the Session Storage.

We can test this code with a couple of users that we will insert into the database:

```
insert into users(firstname, lastname, username, password, role, email, token)
values
('user', 'user', 'user', 'Ln0g6rm/5ZZsk7aiTD4m+u04VvVttKlrTLtlsdUE1FeFdeoT',
  'customer', 'user@test.com', 'xx'),
('admin', 'admin', 'admin', '3hcC1AY+a01PubIStJLoqrBQPkKshQSbmL2qedTFykRc8Ttx',
  'admin', 'admin@test.com', 'xx')
```

LISTING 8-14: **SQL code**

You may find the code for this chapter here:

https://github.com/htset/eshop-angular-18/tree/part8

Credits: This chapter was based on the following posts from Jason Watmore:

https://jasonwatmore.com/post/2020/10/17/angular-10-basic-http-authentication-tutorial-example https://jasonwatmore.com/post/2018/08/14/aspnet-core-21-jwt-authentication-tutorial-with-example-api

9. Authorization

In this chapter, we complement the authentication functionality by introducing authorization to our project.

Frontend

First of all, we add a new folder (named `helpers`) that will contain helper classes for authorization and other stuff.

Inside the `helpers` folder we create an interceptor class:

```
import { Injectable } from "@angular/core";
import { HttpEvent, HttpHandler, HttpInterceptor, HttpRequest }
  from "@angular/common/http";
import { Observable } from "rxjs";
import { environment } from "../../environments/environment";
import { StoreService } from "../services/store.service";

@Injectable()
export class JwtInterceptor implements HttpInterceptor {
  constructor(private storeService: StoreService) { }

  intercept(request: HttpRequest<any>, next: HttpHandler):
    Observable<HttpEvent<any>> {
    const currentUser = this.storeService.user;
    const isLoggedIn = currentUser && currentUser.token;
    const isApiUrl = request.url.startsWith(environment.apiUrl);
    if (isLoggedIn && isApiUrl) {
      request = request.clone({
        setHeaders: {
          Authorization: `Bearer ${currentUser?.token}`
        }
      });
    }
    return next.handle(request);
  }
}
```

LISTING 9-1: *jwt.interceptor.ts*

This class contains a single function that gets called for every outgoing http request (to the API only). If the user has already logged in, this function will add a JSON Web Token in the request header. This token was sent by the backend during the authentication phase and was stored in session storage, as we already saw in the previous chapter.

The token is inspected by the backend API middleware in order to decide whether the request for data is authorized or not.

Make sure you declare the interceptor class in *app.module.ts*:

```
...
  providers: [
    provideAnimationsAsync(),
    {
      provide: HTTP_INTERCEPTORS,
      useClass: JwtInterceptor, multi: true
    }
  ],
...
```

LISTING 9-2: app.module.ts

Next, we create a new folder (src/app/components/admin) that will contain the components for the administration of our application.

Inside the admin folder we create two new components:

- admin-home
- admin-users

The admin-home component contains the menu for the admin pages and provides the router outlet for the display of the other admin components that we will create:

```
<h2>Admin pages</h2>
<nav class="navbar navbar-light"
     style="background-color: #e3f2fd;">
  <a class="nav-item nav-link"
     routerLink="/admin/users">Users</a>
</nav>
<router-outlet></router-outlet>
```

LISTING 9-3: admin-home.component.html

The admin-users component displays info about all users:

```
<h3>Users</h3>
<div class="card-body">
  @if(users){
  <table class="table table-striped">
    <tr>
      <th>ID</th>
      <th>Username</th>
      <th>First Name</th>
      <th>Last Name</th>
      <th>Role</th>
      <th>Email</th>
    </tr>
    @for(user of users; track user.id){
      <tr>
        <td>{{user.id}}</td>
        <td>{{user.username}}</td>
```

```
      <td>{{user.firstName}}</td>
      <td>{{user.lastName}}</td>
      <td>{{user.role}}</td>
      <td>{{user.email}}</td>
    </tr>
  }
  </table>
  }
</div>
```

LISTING 9-4: admin-users.component.html

```
import { Component, OnInit } from '@angular/core';
import { User } from '../../../models/user';
import { UserService } from '../../../services/user.service';

@Component({
  selector: 'app-admin-users',
  templateUrl: './admin-users.component.html',
  styleUrl: './admin-users.component.css'
})
export class AdminUsersComponent implements OnInit {

  users!: User[];

  constructor(private userService: UserService) { }

  ngOnInit() {
    this.userService.getAllUsers().subscribe(
      ((users: User[]) => {
        this.users = users;
      }),
      ((err: any) => {
        console.log(err);
      }));
  }
}
```

LISTING 9-5: admin-users.component.ts

The admin-users component makes use of a new service, UserService that communicates with the backend API:

```
import { HttpClient, HttpHeaders } from '@angular/common/http';
import { Injectable } from '@angular/core';
import { User } from '../models/user';
import { environment } from '../../environments/environment';

@Injectable({
  providedIn: 'root'
})
export class UserService {
```

```
  httpOptions = {
    headers: new HttpHeaders({ 'Content-Type': 'application/json' })
  };

  constructor(private http: HttpClient) { }

  getAllUsers() {
    return this.http.get<User[]>(`${environment.apiUrl}/users`);
  }
}
```

LISTING 9-6: user.service.ts

Access to the admin components should be allowed only to users of type *admin*. We achieve this with the use of a *guard class* (auth.guard.ts), that we create inside the `helpers` folder:

```
import { Injectable } from "@angular/core";
import { ActivatedRouteSnapshot, CanActivate, Router, RouterStateSnapshot }
  from "@angular/router";
import { StoreService } from "../services/store.service";

@Injectable({ providedIn: 'root' })
export class AuthGuard implements CanActivate {
  constructor(
    private router: Router,
    private storeService: StoreService
  ) { }

  canActivate(route: ActivatedRouteSnapshot, state: RouterStateSnapshot) {
    const currentUser = this.storeService.user;
    if (currentUser && currentUser.role == 'admin') {
      return true;
    }
    else if (currentUser && currentUser.role == 'customer') {
      this.router.navigate(['/items']);
      return true;
    }

    this.router.navigate(['/login'], { queryParams: { returnUrl: state.url } });
    return false;
  }
}
```

LISTING 9-7: auth.guard.ts

The `canActivate()` function in the guard class is called whenever access to a protected route is requested. We designate routes as protected in *app-routing.module.ts*:

```
...
const routes: Routes = [
```

```
    { path: '', component: ItemsComponent },
    { path: 'items', component: ItemsComponent },
    { path: 'items/:id', component: ItemDetailsComponent },
    { path: 'cart', component: CartComponent },
    { path: 'login', component: LoginComponent },
    {
      path: 'admin', component: AdminHomeComponent,
        canActivate: [AuthGuard],
      children: [
        { path: 'users', component: AdminUsersComponent }
      ]
    },
];
...
```

LISTING 9-8: app-routing.module.ts

We see that access to the /admin route will result in the invocation of the canActivate() function in AuthGuard class. This function checks whether the user is logged in and of type "admin" and only then allows access to the /admin route.

Note also, the way that we define children routes (e.g. /admin/users). The guard restrictions apply also to all those routes.

Backend

First of all, we are going to create an AppSettings class in the *Helpers* folder and move the secret string there:

```
namespace eshop_angular_18.Server.Helpers
{
  public class AppSettings
  {
    public string Secret { get; set; }
  }
}
```

LISTING 9-9: AppSettings.cs

In this way, we will put the secret in the *appsettings.json* file and avoid hard coding it:

```
  "AppSettings": {
    "Secret": "this is a very long string to be used as secret"
  },
```

LISTING 9-10: appSettings.json

We should modify UserController to get the secret from the AppSettings class:

```csharp
public class UserController : ControllerBase
{
    private readonly EshopContext Context;
    private readonly AppSettings AppSettings;

    public UserController(EshopContext context,
        IOptions<AppSettings> appSettings)
    {
        Context = context;
        AppSettings = appSettings.Value;
    }

....

    private string CreateToken(User user)
    {
        var jwtTokenHandler = new JwtSecurityTokenHandler();
        var key = Encoding.ASCII.GetBytes(AppSettings.Secret);
        var identity = new ClaimsIdentity(new Claim[]
        {
          new Claim(ClaimTypes.Role, user.Role)
        });
        var credentials =
          new SigningCredentials(new SymmetricSecurityKey(key),
            SecurityAlgorithms.HmacSha256);

        var tokenDescriptor = new SecurityTokenDescriptor
        {
          Subject = identity,
          Expires = DateTime.Now.AddMinutes(120),
          SigningCredentials = credentials
        };

        var token = jwtTokenHandler.CreateToken(tokenDescriptor);
        return jwtTokenHandler.WriteToken(token);
    }
}
```

LISTING 9-11: UserController.cs

Now, let's proceed with the JSON Web Token processing. As we saw earlier, each HTTP request to the backend will contain a JWT in the header. The task of the middleware is to extract the Token and verify that it is valid.

In addition to that, the middleware will extract from the token the role of the user (admin or customer). Based on the role, we will be able to authorize or not the access to a specific REST resource.

First of all, we need to install package `Microsoft.AspNetCore.Authentication.JwtBearer` that contains the functionality for JWT handling:

```
Install-Package Microsoft.AspNetCore.Authentication.JwtBearer
```

Next, we configure the Token processing middleware in *Program.cs*:

```
var appSettingsSection = builder.Configuration.GetSection("AppSettings");
builder.Services.Configure<AppSettings>(appSettingsSection);

var appSettings = appSettingsSection.Get<AppSettings>();
var key = Encoding.ASCII.GetBytes(appSettings.Secret);

builder.Services.AddAuthentication(x =>
   {
     x.DefaultAuthenticateScheme = JwtBearerDefaults.AuthenticationScheme;
     x.DefaultChallengeScheme = JwtBearerDefaults.AuthenticationScheme;
   }
)
.AddJwtBearer(x =>
   {
     x.RequireHttpsMetadata = false;
     x.SaveToken = true;
     x.TokenValidationParameters = new TokenValidationParameters
     {
       ValidateIssuerSigningKey = true,
       IssuerSigningKey = new SymmetricSecurityKey(key),
       ValidateIssuer = false,
       ValidateAudience = false,
       RoleClaimType = "role",
       NameClaimType = "name"
     };
     x.MapInboundClaims = false;
   }
);

...

app.UseAuthentication();
app.UseAuthorization();
...
```

LISTING 9-12: Program.cs

Now, let's create the `GetAllUsers()` method in the `Users` Controller, that will provide a list of all users to the Angular frontend:

```
public class UserController : ControllerBase
{
    ....

    [Authorize(Roles = "admin")]
    [HttpGet]
    public async Task<ActionResult<List<User>>> GetAllUsers()
    {
      return await Context.Users
```

```
        .Select(x => new User()
        {
          Id = x.Id,
          FirstName = x.FirstName,
          LastName = x.LastName,
          Username = x.Username,
          Password = null,
          Role = x.Role,
          Email = x.Email
        })
        .ToListAsync();
  }
  ....
}
```

LISTING 9-13: UserController.cs

Note that the class has the `[Authorize]` annotation, stating also that this method can be called only for users that have the "admin" role.

For testing, let's remove temporarily the `canActivate` parameter from file *app-routing.module.ts* in the Angular frontend and try to access directly the `admin/users` page. If we are not logged in, we will get a *401 Unauthorized* error. If we are logged in as customers, then we will get a *403 Forbidden*, which means that we do not have access to this resource.

You may find the code for this chapter here:

https://github.com/htset/eshop-angular-18/tree/part9

Credits: This chapter was based on the following posts by Jason Watmore:

https://jasonwatmore.com/post/2020/10/17/angular-10-basic-http-authentication-tutorial-example

https://jasonwatmore.com/post/2018/08/14/aspnet-core-21-jwt-authentication-tutorial-with-example-api

10. Authentication —Access token refresh/revoke

On this chapter, we will continue with the authentication stuff and we will introduce the functionality to refresh a token upon its expiration. We will also enable the revocation of a token at user logout.

If you study the code about authentication, you will see that the access token has an expiration time of 2 hours, which is a very long time to keep the same token. Tokens should be short-lived and should be refreshed upon expiration, in order to ensure that our application remains secure.

To achieve this, we will use the following process: First of all, we will reduce the access token expiration time to 2 minutes. After the access token has expired, any attempt to access a protected route in the frontend (i.e. the admin part of the application) will result in a request to the API for a token refresh. After the access token has been refreshed successfully, it replaces the existing one, and the process continues until the new token expires as well.

The token refresh operation requires the use of a new kind of token, the refresh token. This is a long random string that will stay the same for a much longer time (e.g. one week). When the frontend needs to refresh the access token, it will send the refresh token to the API as a proof of its identity.

Backend

To start, we modify the User model, by adding the refresh token and its expiration time:

```
namespace eshop_angular_18.Server.Models
{
  public class User
  {
    public int Id { get; set; }
    public string? FirstName { get; set; }
    public string? LastName { get; set; }
    public string? Username { get; set; }
    public string? Password { get; set; }
    public string? Token { get; set; }
    public string? RefreshToken { get; set; }
    public DateTime? RefreshTokenExpiry { get; set; }
    public string? Role { get; set; }
    public string? Email { get; set; }
  }
}
```

LISTING 10-1: User.cs

Then, we modify the corresponding controller (UserController):

```csharp
using eshop_angular_18.Server.Helpers;
using eshop_angular_18.Server.Models;
using Microsoft.AspNetCore.Authorization;
using Microsoft.AspNetCore.Cors;
using Microsoft.AspNetCore.Mvc;
using Microsoft.EntityFrameworkCore;
using Microsoft.Extensions.Options;
using Microsoft.IdentityModel.Tokens;
using System.IdentityModel.Tokens.Jwt;
using System.Security.Claims;
using System.Security.Cryptography;
using System.Text;

namespace eshop_angular_18.Server.Controllers
{
  [Route("api/users")]
  [EnableCors("angular_eshop_AllowSpecificOrigins")]
  [ApiController]
  public class UserController : ControllerBase
  {
    private readonly EshopContext Context;
    private readonly AppSettings AppSettings;

    public UserController(EshopContext context,
        IOptions<AppSettings> appSettings)
    {
      Context = context;
      AppSettings = appSettings.Value;
    }

    [HttpPost("authenticate")]
    public async Task<IActionResult> Authenticate([FromBody] User formParams)
    {
      if (formParams == null || formParams.Password == null)
        return BadRequest(new { message = "Log in failed" });

      var user = await Context.Users
          .SingleOrDefaultAsync(x => x.Username == formParams.Username);

      if (user == null || user.Password == null)
        return BadRequest(new { message = "Log in failed" });

      if (!PasswordHasher
          .VerifyPassword(formParams.Password, user.Password))
        return BadRequest(new { message = "Log in failed" });

      user.Token = CreateToken(user);
      user.RefreshToken = CreateRefreshToken();
      user.RefreshTokenExpiry = DateTime.Now.AddDays(7);
      Context.SaveChanges();

      user.Password = null;

      return Ok(user);
    }
```

```csharp
[Authorize(Roles = "admin")]
[HttpGet]
public async Task<ActionResult<List<User>>> GetAllUsers()
{
  return await Context.Users
      .Select(x => new User()
      {
        Id = x.Id,
        FirstName = x.FirstName,
        LastName = x.LastName,
        Username = x.Username,
        Password = null,
        Role = x.Role,
        Email = x.Email
      })
      .ToListAsync();
}

private string CreateToken(User user)
{
  var jwtTokenHandler = new JwtSecurityTokenHandler();
  var key = Encoding.ASCII.GetBytes(AppSettings.Secret);
  var identity = new ClaimsIdentity(new Claim[]
  {
    new Claim(ClaimTypes.Role, user.Role)
  });
  var credentials
    = new SigningCredentials(new SymmetricSecurityKey(key),
        SecurityAlgorithms.HmacSha256);

  var tokenDescriptor = new SecurityTokenDescriptor
  {
    Subject = identity,
    Expires = DateTime.Now.AddMinutes(2),
    SigningCredentials = credentials
  };

  var token = jwtTokenHandler.CreateToken(tokenDescriptor);
  return jwtTokenHandler.WriteToken(token);
}

private string CreateRefreshToken()
{
  var randomNum = new byte[64];
  using (var generator = RandomNumberGenerator.Create())
  {
    generator.GetBytes(randomNum);
    return Convert.ToBase64String(randomNum);
  }
}

[HttpPost("refresh")]
public async Task<IActionResult> RefreshToken([FromBody] User data)
{
```

```csharp
    var user = await Context.Users
        .SingleOrDefaultAsync(u => (u.RefreshToken == data.RefreshToken)
            && (u.Token == data.Token));

    if (user == null || DateTime.Now > user.RefreshTokenExpiry)
      return BadRequest(new { message = "Invalid token" });

    user.Token = CreateToken(user);
    user.RefreshToken = CreateRefreshToken();
    user.RefreshTokenExpiry = DateTime.Now.AddDays(7);
    Context.SaveChanges();

    user.Password = null;

    return Ok(user);
  }

  [Authorize]
  [HttpPost("revoke")]
  public async Task<IActionResult> RevokeToken([FromBody] User data)
  {
    var user = await Context.Users
        .SingleOrDefaultAsync(u => (u.RefreshToken == data.RefreshToken));

    if (user == null || DateTime.Now > user.RefreshTokenExpiry)
      return BadRequest(new { message = "Invalid token" });

    user.Token = null;
    user.RefreshToken = null;
    user.RefreshTokenExpiry = null;
    Context.SaveChanges();

    user.Password = null;

    return Ok(user);
  }
 }
}
```

LISTING 10-2: UserController.cs

More specifically:

- We modify the `Authenticate()` method, so that it also generates a refresh token. Moreover, we save both tokens in the User entry in the database.
- We change the Token duration to 2 minutes in `CreateToken()`
- We add the `RefreshToken()` method. Here, we verify that the refresh token is valid (and not expired) and we generate a new access token (and a new refresh token as well).
- Finally, we add the `RevokeToken()` method. This is a protected action (note the [Authorize] annotation), where we delete both tokens from the database.

We should not forget to create a new migration, since we have modified the User model, and we are good to go:

`PM>Add-Migration RefreshTokenAdded`

`PM>Update-Database`

Frontend

On the Angular side, we start with updating the User model to reflect the changes in the backend:

```
export class User {
  id?: number;
  username?: string;
  password?: string;
  firstName?: string;
  lastName?: string;
  token?: string;
  refreshToken?: string;
  refreshTokenExpiry?: Date;
  role?: string;
  email?: string;
}
```

LISTING 11-3: user.ts

The bulk of our work takes place in *auth.guard.ts* file:

```
import { Injectable } from "@angular/core";
import { ActivatedRouteSnapshot, CanActivate, Router, RouterStateSnapshot }
  from "@angular/router";
import { StoreService } from "../services/store.service";
import { AuthenticationService } from "../services/authentication.service";
import { lastValueFrom } from "rxjs";

@Injectable({ providedIn: 'root' })
export class AuthGuard implements CanActivate {
  constructor(
    private router: Router,
    private storeService: StoreService,
    private authenticationService: AuthenticationService
  ) { }

  canActivate(route: ActivatedRouteSnapshot,
    state: RouterStateSnapshot) {
    const currentUser = this.storeService.user;
    if (currentUser && currentUser.role == 'admin') {
      if (currentUser.token && !this.tokenExpired(currentUser.token))
        return true;
```

```
      if (!this.refreshToken(currentUser?.token || '',
        currentUser?.refreshToken || '')) {
        this.router.navigate(['/login'],
          { queryParams: { returnUrl: state.url } });
        return false;
      }
      return true;
    }
    else if (currentUser && currentUser.role == 'customer') {
      if (currentUser.token && !this.tokenExpired(currentUser.token)) {
        this.router.navigate(['/items']);
        return true;
      }

      if (!this.refreshToken(currentUser?.token || '',
        currentUser?.refreshToken || '')) {
        this.router.navigate(['/login'],
          { queryParams: { returnUrl: state.url } });
        return false;
      }
      return true;
    }

    this.router.navigate(['/login'],
      { queryParams: { returnUrl: state.url } });
    return false;
  }

  private tokenExpired(token: string) {
    const expiry = (JSON.parse(atob(token.split('.')[1]))).exp;
    return (Math.floor((new Date).getTime() / 1000)) >= expiry;
  }

  private async refreshToken(token: string,
    refreshToken: string): Promise<boolean> {
    try {
      await lastValueFrom(this.authenticationService
        .refreshToken(token, refreshToken));
      return true;
    }
    catch (err) {
      return false;
    }
  }
}
```

LISTING 10-4: auth.guard.ts

When the user tries to access a protected route, function `canActivate()` is called. Here, we check whether the access token has expired. If so, the `refreshToken()` function (from the Authentication service) is called.

In the AuthenticationService class, the corresponding refreshToken() function sends a POST request (/users/refresh) to the API. This request contains the current access and refresh tokens:

```typescript
import { Injectable } from '@angular/core';
import { StoreService } from './store.service';
import { HttpClient } from '@angular/common/http';
import { environment } from '../../environments/environment';
import { map } from 'rxjs';
import { User } from '../models/user';

@Injectable({
  providedIn: 'root'
})
export class AuthenticationService {

  constructor(
    public storeService: StoreService,
    private http: HttpClient
  ) { }

  login(username: string, password: string) {
    return this.http.post<User>(`${environment.apiUrl}/users/authenticate`,
      { username, password })
      .pipe(
        map(user => {
          sessionStorage.setItem('user', JSON.stringify(user));
          this.storeService.user = user;
          return user;
        })
      );
  }

  logout(refreshToken: string) {
    this.http.post<any>(`${environment.apiUrl}/users/revoke`,
      { refreshToken })
      .subscribe();

    sessionStorage.removeItem('user');
    this.storeService.user = null;
  }

  refreshToken(token: string, refreshToken: string) {
    return this.http.post<User>(`${environment.apiUrl}/users/refresh`,
      { token, refreshToken })
      .pipe(
        map(user => {
          sessionStorage.setItem('user', JSON.stringify(user));
          this.storeService.user = user;
          return user;
        })
      );
  }
}
```

LISTING 10-5: authentication.service.ts

You may also note here, that the `logout()` function has been modified. Apart from removing the current user from session storage, it also sends a POST request (`/users/revoke`) to the API. This function is called from `AppComponent` class when the user clicks on Log out:

```typescript
import { Component } from '@angular/core';
import { StoreService } from './services/store.service';
import { AuthenticationService } from './services/authentication.service';
import { Router } from '@angular/router';
import { User } from './models/user';

@Component({
  selector: 'app-root',
  templateUrl: './app.component.html',
  styleUrls: ['./app.component.css']
})
export class AppComponent {

  user: User | null = null;

  constructor(
    private router: Router,
    public authenticationService: AuthenticationService,
    public storeService: StoreService
  ) {
    this.storeService.user$.subscribe(x => this.user = x);
  }

  logout(e: Event) {
    e.preventDefault();
    const currentUser = this.storeService.user;
    this.authenticationService.logout(currentUser?.refreshToken || '');
    this.router.navigate(['/login']);
  }
}
```

LISTING 10-6: app.component.ts

Now, the access token expires every 2 minutes. When the user tries to access a protected route, the token is refreshed automatically for 2 more minutes, keeping the user logged in.

You may find the code for this chapter here:

https://github.com/htset/eshop-angular-18/tree/part10

11. Checkout

In this chapter, we will implement the first part of the checkout functionality. In this page, the customer gets a summary of the selected items in the cart and enters the delivery address. The user may add a new address, or select a previously selected one, that has been stored in the database during a previous purchase.

Here, we will see how to use *signals* in our code as well as how to make a component that is used by another component, and how those two components interact. Furthermore, we will see again how to create reactive forms in our components.

Frontend

Let's start with the introduction of the `Address` model:

```
export interface Address {
  id: number;
  userId: number
  firstName: string;
  lastName: string;
  street: string;
  zip: string;
  city: string;
  country: string;
}
```

LISTING 11-1: address.ts

Next, we create the delivery-address component that will enable users to select an existing delivery address or create a new one. Users will also be able to modify an existing address or delete it altogether.

The new component is created in the `shared` folder, as it a general-purpose component that may be used also in other contexts:

```
<form [formGroup]="addressForm" (ngSubmit)="onSubmit()">
  <div class="form-group">
    <label for="firstname">First Name:</label>
    <input type="text"
           class="form-control form-control-sm" formControlName="firstName" />
  </div>
  <div class="form-group">
    <label for="lastname">Last Name:</label>
    <input type="text"
           class="form-control form-control-sm" formControlName="lastName" />
  </div>
  <div class="form-group">
    <label for="street">Street:</label>
    <input type="text"
```

```html
                class="form-control form-control-sm" formControlName="street" />
      </div>
      <div class="form-group">
        <label for="zip">ZIP code:</label>
        <input type="text"
                class="form-control form-control-sm" formControlName="zip" />
      </div>
      <div class="form-group">
        <label for="city">City:</label>
        <input type="text"
                class="form-control form-control-sm" formControlName="city" />
      </div>
      <div class="form-group">
        <label for="country">Country:</label>
        <input type="text"
                class="form-control form-control-sm" formControlName="country" />
      </div>
      <button type="submit"
              class="btn btn-primary" [disabled]="!addressForm.valid">
        Save
      </button>
</form>
```

LISTING 11-2: delivery-address.component.html

The delivery-address component consists of a reactive form. The form is controlled by the addressForm form group. This form group contains a number of form controls that correspond to the text inputs presented in the template:

```typescript
import { Component, OnInit, model } from '@angular/core';
import { Address } from '../../../models/address';
import { FormControl, FormGroup, Validators } from '@angular/forms';

@Component({
  selector: 'app-delivery-address',
  templateUrl: './delivery-address.component.html',
  styleUrl: './delivery-address.component.css'
})
export class DeliveryAddressComponent implements OnInit {

  address = model<Address>();

  addressForm = new FormGroup({
    firstName: new FormControl('', Validators.required),
    lastName: new FormControl('', Validators.required),
    street: new FormControl('', Validators.required),
    zip: new FormControl('', Validators.required),
    city: new FormControl('', Validators.required),
    country: new FormControl('', Validators.required),
    id: new FormControl(''),
    userId: new FormControl('')
  });
```

```
  constructor() { }

  ngOnInit(): void {
    if (this.address !== undefined) {
      this.addressForm.controls
        .firstName.setValue(this.address()?.firstName || '');
      this.addressForm.controls
        .lastName.setValue(this.address()?.lastName || '');
      this.addressForm.controls
        .street.setValue(this.address()?.street || '');
      this.addressForm.controls
        .zip.setValue(this.address()?.zip || '');
      this.addressForm.controls
        .city.setValue(this.address()?.city || '');
      this.addressForm.controls
        .country.setValue(this.address()?.country || '');
      this.addressForm.controls
        .id.setValue(this.address()?.id.toString() || '0');
      this.addressForm.controls.
        userId.setValue(this.address()?.userId.toString() || '0');
    }
  }

  onSubmit() {
    var addr: Address = {
      firstName: this.addressForm.value.firstName || '',
      lastName: this.addressForm.value.lastName || '',
      street: this.addressForm.value.street || '',
      zip: this.addressForm.value.zip || '',
      city: this.addressForm.value.city || '',
      country: this.addressForm.value.country || '',
      id: parseInt(this.addressForm.value.id || '0'),
      userId: parseInt(this.addressForm.value.userId || '0')
    }

    this.address.set(addr);
  }
}
```

LISTING 11-3: delivery-address.component.ts

In reactive forms, the form model is the source of truth. This means that the form controls contain the information about the delivery address, and that they provide this information to the input boxes, through the `formControl` directive.

The delivery-address component will be inserted into another component that we will create next, the *checkout* component. The host component informs the child component of a preselected address to be displayed, by using a `model` signal.

In turn, after we submit the form, the child component informs the host component of the new address, by emitting an event. This event can be captured in the parent component by listening for an event whose name is the name of the model variable suffixed by "Change". In our case, the name of the event is addressChange.

Let's now create the checkout component:

```
<h2>Checkout</h2>

@if(storeService.cart.cartItems.length > 0){
<div class="card">
  <div class="card-body" id="cartBody">
    <h3 class="card-header">Cart</h3>
    <table class="table table-striped">
      <tr>
        <th>Item name</th>
        <th>Quantity</th>
        <th>Unit Price</th>
        <th>Total Price</th>
      </tr>
      @for(ci of storeService.cart.cartItems; track ci){
      <tr>
        <td>{{ci.item.name}}</td>
        <td>{{ci.quantity}}</td>
        <td>{{ci.item.price}}</td>
        <td>{{ci.item.price * ci.quantity}}</td>
      </tr>
      }
    </table>
    Cart Total: {{storeService.cart.getTotalValue()}}
  </div>
</div>
}

@if(storeService.cart.cartItems.length == 0){
<div class="card">
  <div class="card-body" id="noCartBody">
    <h3 class="card-header">Cart</h3>
    Cart is empty
  </div>
</div>
}

@if(storeService.user?.id){
<div class="card">
  <div class="card-body" id="addressBody">
    <h3 class="card-header">Delivery Address</h3>
    <form (ngSubmit)="onSubmit()">
      <table style="width:100%;">
        @for(addr of addressList(); track addr){
        <tr>
          <td style="vertical-align: top;">
            <input type="radio"
                   id="selectedAddress{{addr.id}}"
                   name="selectedAddress"
                   [value]="addr.id"
                   [ngModel]="selectedAddressId()"
```

```
            (change)="selectionChanged($any($event.target).id)"/>
    </td>

    @if(addressIdForModification() != addr.id){
    <td>
      <strong>{{addr.firstName + ' ' + addr.lastName}}</strong><br />
      {{addr.street}} <br />
      {{addr.zip + ' ' + addr.city}}<br />
      {{addr.country}} <br />
    </td>
    }

    @if(addressIdForModification() == addr.id){
    <td>
      <app-delivery-address
        (addressChange)="addressChanged($event)"
        [address]="addr">
      </app-delivery-address>
    </td>
    }

    <td style="vertical-align: top;">
      @if(addressIdForModification() != addr.id){
      <button type="button"
              id="modify{{addr.id}}"
              (click)="modifyAddress(addr)">
        Modify
      </button>
      }

      @if(addressIdForModification() == addr.id){
      <button type="button"
              id="cancel{{addr.id}}"
              (click)="cancelModifyAddress()">
        Cancel
      </button>
      }

      <br />
      @if(addressIdForModification() != addr.id){
      <button type="button"
              (click)="deleteAddress(addr)">
        Delete
      </button>
      }
    </td>
  </tr>
  }
  <tr>
    <td style="vertical-align: top;">
      <input type="radio"
             id="selectedAddress0"
             name="selectedAddress"
             [value]="0"
             [ngModel]="selectedAddressId()"
```

```html
                    (change)="selectionChanged($any($event.target).id)"/>
          </td>
          <td>
            <strong>New address:</strong><br />
            @if(selectedAddressId() == 0){
            <app-delivery-address
              (addressChange)="addressChanged($event)">
            </app-delivery-address>
            }
          </td>
        </tr>
      </table>
      <input type="submit"
             id="toPayment"
             [disabled]="!((addressIdForModification()       ==       -1)       &&
(selectedAddressId() > 0) && (storeService.cart.cartItems.length > 0))"
             value="To payment" />
    </form>
  </div>
</div>
}

@if(!storeService.user?.id){
  <div class="card">
    <div class="card-body" id="loginLink">
      <h3 class="card-header">Delivery Address</h3>
      <p>
        You need to <a [routerLink]="['/login']"
                       [queryParams]="{returnUrl: 'checkout'}">log in</a>
      </p>
    </div>
  </div>
}

<button routerLink="/cart">Back to Cart</button>
<br />
```

LISTING 11-4: checkout.component.html

The template can be divided in two parts. On the top half, a summary of the shopping cart contents is provided.

On the bottom half (and only if the customer has logged in), we display (using an @for loop) the already available delivery addresses for the current user, as retrieved from the database. We also provide the option for the user to insert a new address. In both cases, we use the *delivery-address* component and we pass as parameters the event handler for the addressChange and the address to be used for display each time (this will be assigned to the model signal in the child component).

The user is also able to modify a selected delivery address, as well as delete the address from the database. Here is the code for the component:

```typescript
import { Component, OnInit, signal } from '@angular/core';
import { Address } from '../../../models/address';
import { StoreService } from '../../../services/store.service';
import { UserService } from '../../../services/user.service';
import { Router } from '@angular/router';
import { mergeMap, tap } from 'rxjs';

@Component({
  selector: 'app-checkout',
  templateUrl: './checkout.component.html',
  styleUrl: './checkout.component.css'
})
export class CheckoutComponent implements OnInit {

  addressIdForModification = signal<number>(-1);
  selectedAddressId = signal<number>(-1);
  addressList = signal<Address[]>([]);

  constructor(public storeService: StoreService,
    public userService: UserService,
    public router: Router) { }

  ngOnInit(): void {
    if (this?.storeService?.user?.id || 0 > 0) {
      //get addresses already saved by user
      this.userService
        .getAddressByUserId(this?.storeService?.user?.id || 0)
        .subscribe(addresses => {
          this.addressList.set(addresses);
          this.selectedAddressId.set(this.storeService.deliveryAddress);
        })
    }
  }

  selectionChanged(elementId: string): void {
    //elementId contains the ID of the selected address
    this.selectedAddressId.set(parseInt(elementId.
      substring(15, elementId.length)));
  }

  //function that is passed to the DeliveryAddress component
  addressChanged(addr: Address | undefined): void {
    let newAddress: Address;
    if (addr !== undefined) {
      addr.userId = this?.storeService?.user?.id || 0;

      if (this?.storeService?.user?.id || 0 > 0) {
        //save address in DB
        this.userService.saveAddress(addr).pipe(
          tap(res => newAddress = res),
          mergeMap(res => this.userService
            .getAddressByUserId(this?.storeService?.user?.id || 0))
        )
          .subscribe(addresses => {
            this.addressList.set(addresses);
```

```typescript
          //change selected checkbox
          this.selectedAddressId.set(newAddress.id || 0);
          //toggle modifying
          this.addressIdForModification.set(-1);
        })
      }
    }
  }

  modifyAddress(addr: Address): void {
    this.addressIdForModification.set(addr.id || -1);
  }

  cancelModifyAddress(): void {
    this.addressIdForModification.set(-1);
  }

  deleteAddress(addr: Address): void {
    if (this?.storeService?.user?.id || 0 > 0) {
      this.userService.deleteAddress(addr.id)
        .subscribe(addressId => {
          this.addressList.set(this.addressList()
            ?.filter(addr => addr.id != addressId));

          if (this.selectedAddressId() == addressId)
            this.selectedAddressId.set(-1);
        })
    }
  }

  onSubmit(): void {
    this.storeService.deliveryAddress = this.selectedAddressId();
    this.router.navigate(['/payment']);
  }
}
```

LISTING 11-5: checkout.component.ts

The most interesting part of this code is the event handler `addressChanged()`. Here, we use `mergeMap` to run the `saveAddress` and `getAddressByUserId` operations in sequence, and to avoid placing one `subscribe` method into the other.

Note also that we are using 3 signals for our class members instead of JavaScript properties. Also note in the template, how we bind such a signal to an input:

```html
<input type="radio"
  id="selectedAddress{{addr.id}}"
  name="selectedAddress"
  [value]="addr.id"
  [ngModel]="selectedAddressId()"
  (change)="selectionChanged($any($event.target).id)"/>
```

LISTING 11-6: checkout.component html

The checkout component makes use of address-handling functions defined in `UserService`. Those functions make HTTP calls to the backend API:

```
import { HttpClient, HttpHeaders } from '@angular/common/http';
import { Injectable } from '@angular/core';
import { User } from '../models/user';
import { environment } from '../../environments/environment';
import { Address } from '../models/address';

@Injectable({
  providedIn: 'root'
})
export class UserService {

  httpOptions = {
    headers: new HttpHeaders({ 'Content-Type': 'application/json' })
  };

  constructor(private http: HttpClient) { }

  getAllUsers() {
    return this.http.get<User[]>(`${environment.apiUrl}/users`);
  }

  getAddressByUserId(userId: number) {
    return this.http.get<Address[]>(`${environment.apiUrl}/address`);
  }

  saveAddress(address: Address) {
    return this.http.post<Address>(`${environment.apiUrl}/address`, address);
  }

  deleteAddress(addressId?: number) {
    return this.http.delete<number>(`${environment.apiUrl}/address/${addressId}`);
  }
}
```

LISTING 11-7: user.service.ts

Note also that we have added the currently selected delivery address ID into `StoreService`:

```
...
  private readonly _deliveryAddress = new BehaviorSubject<number>(-1);
  readonly deliveryAddress$ = this._deliveryAddress.asObservable();

  get deliveryAddress(): number {
    return this._deliveryAddress.getValue();
  }
```

```
  set deliveryAddress(val: number) {
    this._deliveryAddress.next(val);
  }
...
```

LISTING 11-8: store.service.ts

Finally, we need a routing entry in *app-routing.module.ts*, so that we can navigate from the cart to the checkout component:

```
...
const routes: Routes = [
  { path: '', component: ItemsComponent },
  { path: 'items', component: ItemsComponent },
  { path: 'items/:id', component: ItemDetailsComponent },
  { path: 'cart', component: CartComponent },
  { path: 'checkout', component: CheckoutComponent },
  { path: 'login', component: LoginComponent },
  {
    path: 'admin', component: AdminHomeComponent,
    canActivate: [AuthGuard],
    children: [
      {
        path: 'users', component: AdminUsersComponent,
        canActivate: [AuthGuard]
      }
    ]
  },
];
...
```

LISTING 11-9: app-routing.module.ts

Backend

Let's move now to the ASP.NET Web API project. First, we introduce the model for the delivery address:

```
namespace eshop_angular_18.Server.Models
{
  public class Address
  {
    public int Id { get; set; }
    public int UserId { get; set; }
    public string? FirstName { get; set; }
    public string? LastName { get; set; }
    public string? Street { get; set; }
    public string? Zip { get; set; }
    public string? City { get; set; }
    public string? Country { get; set; }
  }
}
```

LISTING 11-10: Address.cs

Next, we create a new WebAPI controller, `AddressController` that contains CRUD functionality for the handling of delivery addresses:

```
using eshop_angular_18.Server.Models;
using Microsoft.AspNetCore.Cors;
using Microsoft.AspNetCore.Mvc;
using Microsoft.EntityFrameworkCore;

namespace eshop_angular_18.Server.Controllers
{
  [Route("api/[controller]")]
  [EnableCors("angular_eshop_AllowSpecificOrigins")]
  [ApiController]
  public class AddressController : ControllerBase
  {
    private readonly EshopContext _context;

    public AddressController(EshopContext context)
    {
      _context = context;
    }

    [HttpGet]
    public async Task<ActionResult<IEnumerable<Address>>> Get()
    {
      return await _context.Addresses.ToListAsync();
    }

    [HttpGet("{userId}")]
    public async Task<ActionResult<IEnumerable<Address>>> GetByUserId(int userId)
    {
      return await _context.Addresses.Where((addr)
          => addr.UserId == userId).ToListAsync();
    }

    [HttpPost]
    public async Task<ActionResult<Address>> Post([FromBody] Address value)
    {
      if (value.Id == 0)
      {
        await _context.Addresses.AddAsync(value);
      }
      else
      {
        _context.Addresses.Update(value);
      }
      await _context.SaveChangesAsync();
      return value;
    }
```

```
    [HttpDelete("{id}")]
    public async Task<int> Delete(int id)
    {
      var addr = await _context.Addresses.FindAsync(id);
      if(addr != null)
      {
        _context.Addresses.Remove(addr);
        await _context.SaveChangesAsync();
      }
      return id;
    }
  }
}
```
LISTING 11-11: AddressController.cs

We also have to modify `EshopContext`, so that it can be aware about addresses too:

```
using Microsoft.EntityFrameworkCore;

namespace eshop_angular_18.Server.Models
{
  public class EshopContext : DbContext
  {
    public EshopContext(DbContextOptions<EshopContext> options)
        : base(options)
    {
    }

    public DbSet<Item> Items { get; set; }
    public DbSet<User> Users { get; set; }
    public DbSet<Address> Addresses { get; set; }

    protected override void OnModelCreating(ModelBuilder modelBuilder)
    {
      modelBuilder.Entity<Item>().Property(p =>
          p.Price).HasColumnType("decimal(18,2)");
    }
  }
}
```

LISTING 11-12: EshopContext.cs

Finally, we add a new migration, in order to create the Addresses table in our database:

PM> add-migration AddressAdded

PM> update-database

In the next chapter, we will continue with the payment and order placing functionality. You may find the code for this chapter here:

https://github.com/htset/eshop-angular-18/tree/part12

12. Order validation and submission

In the previous chapter, we created the checkout page, where the customer views a summary of the cart and selects the delivery address. Here, we will finish the checkout process, by submitting the order to the backend. We will also see how to perform validation, both on the frontend and the backend.

Frontend

We start by creating the models that we will use for the order submission. We define the Order, OrderDetail and CreditCard classes:

```
export class OrderDetail {
  public id?: number;
  public orderId?: number;
  public itemId?: number;
  public itemName?: string;
  public itemUnitPrice?: number;
  public quantity?: number;
  public totalPrice?: number;
}
```

LISTING 12-1: orderDetail.ts

```
export class CreditCard {
  cardNumber?: string;
  holderName?: string;
  code?: string;
  expiryMonth?: number;
  expiryYear?: number;
}
```

LISTING 12-2: creditCard.ts

```
import { CreditCard } from "./creditCard";
import { OrderDetail } from "./orderDetail";

export class Order {
  public id?: number;
  public userId?: number;
  public orderDate?: Date;
  public orderDetails?: OrderDetail[];
  public totalPrice?: number;
  public creditCard?: CreditCard;
  public deliveryAddressId?: number;
  public firstName?: string;
  public lastName?: string;
  public street?: string;
  public zip?: string;
```

```
  public city?: string;
  public country?: string;
}
```

LISTING 12-3: order.ts

Next, we create a new component (payment) that will be the next page in the process of checkout. In this component, after the customer enters her credit card details and presses on *Finalize Order*, the order is submitted to the backend.

The payment component consists of a reactive form that is controlled in the component by a FormGroup object. During the definition of the FormGroup, we can select validation options on each of the associated FormControl objects.

```
import { Component, Input, OnInit } from '@angular/core';
import { AbstractControl, FormControl, FormGroup, Validators }
  from '@angular/forms';
import { Router } from '@angular/router';
import { Cart } from '../../../../app/models/cart';
import { Order } from '../../../../app/models/order';
import { OrderDetail } from '../../../../app/models/orderDetail';
import { OrderService } from '../../../../app/services/order.service';
import { StoreService } from '../../../../app/services/store.service';

@Component({
  selector: 'app-payment',
  templateUrl: './payment.component.html',
  styleUrls: ['./payment.component.css']
})
export class PaymentComponent implements OnInit {
  currentYear:number = new Date().getFullYear();

  paymentForm = new FormGroup({
    cardNumber: new FormControl('',
      [Validators.required, Validators.pattern(/^[0-9]{16}$/)]),
    holderName: new FormControl('',
      Validators.required),
    code: new FormControl('',
      [Validators.required, Validators.pattern(/^[0-9]{3}$/)]),
    expiryMonth: new FormControl('',
      Validators.required),
    expiryYear: new FormControl('',
      Validators.required)
  }, [ValidateExpirationDate]);

  constructor(public storeService: StoreService,
    private orderService: OrderService,
    private router: Router) { }

  ngOnInit(): void { }

  onSubmit(): void {
```

```
    let userId = this?.storeService?.user?.id || 0;
    if (userId > 0) {
      //if user is logged in
      let order: Order = new Order();
      order.userId = userId;
      order.orderDetails = this.storeService
        .cart.cartItems
        .map(
          (cartItem) => {
            let orderDetail: OrderDetail = new OrderDetail();
            orderDetail.itemId = cartItem.item.id;
            orderDetail.quantity = cartItem.quantity;
            return orderDetail;
          });
      order.deliveryAddressId = this.storeService.deliveryAddress;
      order.creditCard = {
        cardNumber:
          this.paymentForm.controls.cardNumber.value || '',
        holderName:
          this.paymentForm.controls.holderName.value || '',
        code:
          this.paymentForm.controls.code.value || '',
        expiryMonth:
          parseInt(this.paymentForm.controls.expiryMonth.value || '0'),
        expiryYear:
          parseInt(this.paymentForm.controls.expiryYear.value || '0'),
    };

      //Submit order
      this.orderService.addOrder(order)
        .subscribe((orderResult: Order) => {
          this.storeService.order = orderResult;
          this.storeService.cart = new Cart();
          this.storeService.deliveryAddress = -1;

          this.router.navigate(['/summary']);
        })
    }
  }

  //creates a sequence of months
  numSequence(n: number): Array<number> {
    return Array(n);
  }

  //creates a sequence of years
  numSequenceStart(n: number, startFrom: number): number[] {
    return [...Array(n).keys()].map(i => i + startFrom);
  }
}

//Custom validator for the expiration date
function ValidateExpirationDate(control: AbstractControl)
  : { [key: string]: any } | null {
  if (control?.get("expiryMonth")?.value && control?.get("expiryYear")?.value) {
```

```
    let month: number = parseInt(control?.get("expiryMonth")?.value);
    let year: number = parseInt(control?.get("expiryYear")?.value);
    let currentDate = new Date();
    if (year < currentDate.getFullYear())
      return { 'CreditCardExpired': true };
    else if (year == currentDate.getFullYear()
      && month - 1 < currentDate.getMonth())
      return { 'CreditCardExpired': true };
  }
  return null;
}
```

LISTING 12-4: payment.component.ts

Apart from the Validators.required option for all controls, we use a regex pattern validation for the Card Number and CVV code text boxes. In this way, we can assure that they consist of 16 and 3 numbers respectively. The credit card validation is a very trivial one, as those numbers are in reality validated with the use of an algorithm.

There are libraries that we can use for this, but it is out of the scope of this book. In most cases anyway, we won't even need to add a credit card details in our project; instead, we will redirect the customer to a specialized credit card processing page (e.g. from a bank).

Here we choose to deal with a more interesting case, the validation of more than one element on the same time. We have to ensure that the credit card has not expired; for that we need to write a custom validator function (validateExpirationDate) that accesses those two text boxes and checks them against the current month and year. This validator is not applied to either element, but on the form group instead.

On the template side, we have inserted suitable error messages under each element. The containing divs will appear when there is an error on the respective element, but only after the element has been touched or changed by the user. The submit button will become enabled when the whole formGroup passes validation:

```
<h2>Payment</h2>

@if(storeService.cart.cartItems.length > 0){
<div class="card">
  <div class="card-body" id="cartBody">
    <h3 class="card-header">Credit card details</h3>

    <form [formGroup]="paymentForm" (ngSubmit)="onSubmit()">
      <div class="form-row">
        <div class="form-group col-md-2">
          <label for="cardNumber">Credit card no.:</label>
          <input type="text" class="form-control form-control-sm"
              formControlName="cardNumber" />
          @if(paymentForm.controls['cardNumber'].invalid
            && (paymentForm.controls['cardNumber'].dirty
              || paymentForm.controls['cardNumber'].touched)){
```

```
      <div class="text-danger">
        @if(paymentForm.controls['cardNumber'].errors){
        <div>
          Please enter a valid credit card number
        </div>
        }
      </div>
      }
    </div>
</div>
<div class="form-row">
  <div class="form-group col-md-2">
    <label for="holderName">Holder's Name:</label>
    <input type="text" class="form-control form-control-sm"
           formControlName="holderName" />
    @if(paymentForm.controls['holderName'].invalid
      && (paymentForm.controls['holderName'].dirty
        || paymentForm.controls['holderName'].touched)){
    <div class="text-danger">
      @if(paymentForm.controls['holderName'].errors){
      <div>
        Please enter the card holder's name
      </div>
      }
    </div>
    }
  </div>
</div>
<div class="form-row">
  <div class="form-group col-md-2">
    <label for="code">CVV Code:</label>
    <input type="text" class="form-control form-control-sm"
           formControlName="code" />
    @if(paymentForm.controls['code'].invalid
      && (paymentForm.controls['code'].dirty
        || paymentForm.controls['code'].touched)){
    <div class="text-danger">
      @if(paymentForm.controls['code'].errors){
      <div>
        Please enter a valid CVV code
      </div>
      }
    </div>
    }
  </div>
</div>
<div class="form-row">
  <div class="form-group col-sm-1">
    <label for="expirydate">Expiry date:</label>
    <select formControlName="expiryMonth"
            class="form-control form-control-sm">
      @for(i of numSequence(12); track $index){
      <option [value]="$index+1">
        {{$index+1}}
      </option>
```

```
              }
            </select>
          </div>
          <div class="form-group col-sm-1">
            <label for="expirydate"> </label>
            <select formControlName="expiryYear"
                    class="form-control form-control-sm">
              @for(i of numSequenceStart(5, currentYear); track i){
              <option [value]="i">
                {{i}}
              </option>
              }
            </select>
          </div>
        </div>
        <div class="form-row">
          @if((paymentForm.controls['expiryMonth'].invalid
              || paymentForm.controls['expiryYear'].invalid)
             && (paymentForm.controls['expiryMonth'].dirty
              || paymentForm.controls['expiryMonth'].touched
              || paymentForm.controls['expiryYear'].dirty
              || paymentForm.controls['expiryYear'].touched)){
          <div class="text-danger">
            @if(paymentForm.controls['expiryMonth'].errors
              || paymentForm.controls['expiryYear'].errors){
            <div>
              Please enter the card's expiration date
            </div>
            }
          </div>
          }

          @if((paymentForm.invalid)
             && (paymentForm.controls['expiryMonth'].dirty
              || paymentForm.controls['expiryMonth'].touched
              || paymentForm.controls['expiryYear'].dirty
              || paymentForm.controls['expiryYear'].touched)){
          <div class="text-danger">
            @if(paymentForm.errors){
            <div>
              The credit card has expired
            </div>
            }
          </div>
          }
        </div>

        <button type="submit"
                [disabled]="!paymentForm.valid">
          Finalize Order
        </button>
      </form>

    </div>
</div>
```

```
}

@if(storeService.cart.cartItems.length == 0){
<div class="card">
  <div class="card-body" id="noCartBody">
    <h3 class="card-header">Cart</h3>
    Cart is empty
  </div>
</div>
}

<button routerLink="/checkout">Back to Checkout</button>
<br />
```

LISTING 12-5: payment.component.html

When submit is clicked and after all validations have passed, a new Order object is created. It is then filled with OrderDetail objects that correspond to the entries in the cart. The order is sent to the backend through the newly created OrderService:

```
import { HttpClient, HttpHeaders } from '@angular/common/http';
import { Injectable } from '@angular/core';
import { Order } from '../models/order';
import { environment } from '../../environments/environment';

@Injectable({
  providedIn: 'root'
})
export class OrderService {

  httpOptions = {
    headers: new HttpHeaders({ 'Content-Type': 'application/json' })
  };
  constructor(private http: HttpClient) { }

  addOrder(order: Order) {
    return this.http
      .post<Order>(`${environment.apiUrl}/order`, order);
  }
}
```

LISTING 12-6: order.service.ts

If the submission is successful, we will be redirected to a new component, called Summary:

```
<p>Order successfully submitted</p>
<p>An email has been sent to: {{this.storeService.user?.email}}</p>
<p>Return to <a routerLink='/'>Items</a> page</p>
```

LISTING 12-7: summary.component.html

```typescript
import { Component, OnInit } from '@angular/core';
import { StoreService } from '../../../services/store.service';
import { User } from '../../../models/user';


@Component({
  selector: 'app-summary',
  templateUrl: './summary.component.html',
  styleUrls: ['./summary.component.css']
})
export class SummaryComponent implements OnInit {

  public userInOrder?: User;
  constructor(public storeService: StoreService) { }

  ngOnInit(): void {
  }
}
```

LISTING 12-8: summary.component.ts

The returned Order object is stored in the StoreService object, for use in subsequent steps:

```typescript
...
  private readonly _order = new BehaviorSubject<Order>(new Order());
  readonly order$ = this._order.asObservable();

  get order(): Order {
    return this._order.getValue();
  }

  set order(val: Order) {
    this._order.next(val);
  }
...
```

LISTING 12-9: store.service.ts

Finally, we should not forget to add the necessary routing entry into *app-routing.module.ts*:

```typescript
...
  {path: 'payment', component: PaymentComponent},
  {path: 'summary', component: SummaryComponent},
...
```

LISTING 12-10: app-routing.module.ts

Backend

On the API side, we will create a new Controller that will take care of the orders submission:

```csharp
using eshop_angular_18.Server.Models;
```

```csharp
using Microsoft.AspNetCore.Mvc;

namespace eshop_angular_18.Server.Controllers
{
  [Route("api/[controller]")]
  [ApiController]
  public class OrderController : ControllerBase
  {
    private readonly EshopContext _context;

    public OrderController(EshopContext context)
    {
      _context = context;
    }

    [HttpGet("{id}")]
    public async Task<ActionResult<Item>> GetOrder(int id)
    {
      var order = await this._context.Orders.FindAsync(id);
      return Ok(order);
    }

    [HttpPost]
    public async Task<ActionResult<Item>> Post([FromBody] OrderDTO dto)
    {
      try
      {
        var NewOrder = await CreateOrderFromDTO(dto);

        if (!TryValidateModel(NewOrder, nameof(Order)))
        {
          return BadRequest(ModelState);
        }

        await this._context.Orders.AddAsync(NewOrder);
        await this._context.SaveChangesAsync();

        var returnDTO = CreateDTOFromOrder(NewOrder);
        return CreatedAtAction(nameof(GetOrder),
          new { id = returnDTO.Id }, returnDTO);
      }
      catch (Exception ex)
      {
        return BadRequest();
      }
    }

    private async Task<Order> CreateOrderFromDTO(OrderDTO dto)
    {
      var NewOrder = new Order();
      NewOrder.OrderDetails = new List<OrderDetail>();

      NewOrder.UserId = dto.UserId;
      NewOrder.OrderDate = DateTime.Now;
```

```csharp
    var tempAddr = await this._context.Addresses
      .FindAsync(dto.DeliveryAddressId);
    NewOrder.FirstName = tempAddr.FirstName;
    NewOrder.LastName = tempAddr.LastName;
    NewOrder.Street = tempAddr.Street;
    NewOrder.Zip = tempAddr.Zip;
    NewOrder.City = tempAddr.City;
    NewOrder.Country = tempAddr.Country;

    decimal tempTotalPrice = 0;
    foreach (var detail in dto.OrderDetails)
    {
      var NewOrderDetail = new OrderDetail();
      var tempItem = await this._context.Items.FindAsync(detail.ItemId);
      NewOrderDetail.ItemId = detail.ItemId;
      NewOrderDetail.ItemName = tempItem.Name;
      NewOrderDetail.ItemUnitPrice = tempItem.Price;
      NewOrderDetail.Quantity = detail.Quantity;
      NewOrderDetail.TotalPrice = tempItem.Price * detail.Quantity;

      NewOrder.OrderDetails.Add(NewOrderDetail);
      tempTotalPrice += NewOrderDetail.TotalPrice;
    }
    NewOrder.TotalPrice = tempTotalPrice;
    return NewOrder;
}

private OrderDTO CreateDTOFromOrder(Order order)
{
    var dto = new OrderDTO();
    dto.OrderDetails = new List<OrderDetailDTO>();

    dto.Id = order.Id;
    dto.UserId = order.UserId;
    dto.OrderDate = order.OrderDate;

    dto.FirstName = order.FirstName;
    dto.LastName = order.LastName;
    dto.Street = order.Street;
    dto.Zip = order.Zip;
    dto.City = order.City;
    dto.Country = order.Country;

    foreach (var detail in order.OrderDetails)
    {
      var dtoDetail = new OrderDetailDTO();
      dtoDetail.Id = detail.Id;
      dtoDetail.OrderId = detail.OrderId;
      dtoDetail.ItemId = detail.ItemId;
      dtoDetail.ItemName = detail.ItemName;
      dtoDetail.ItemUnitPrice = detail.ItemUnitPrice;
      dtoDetail.Quantity = detail.Quantity;
      dtoDetail.TotalPrice = detail.TotalPrice;

      dto.OrderDetails.Add(dtoDetail);
```

```
      }
      dto.TotalPrice = order.TotalPrice;
      return dto;
    }

  }
}
```

LISTING 12-11: OrderController.cs

The important stuff is in the Post method. The controller receives the submitted order in the form of a Data Transfer Object (DTO). Then, it uses the DTO to create the full Order object that will be eventually stored in the database. At the end, a new DTO-containing the newly assigned order and order detail IDs from the database- is returned to the frontend in a *201 (Created)* Response.

We could use the same object for data transfer and data storage, and in simple applications this is the way to go. In more complex applications, it's better to have a DTO that will contain only the information that is exchanged between frontend and backend. Here, although this is not much of a complex app, we opt to go with the DTO solution:

```
using System.ComponentModel.DataAnnotations;

namespace eshop_angular_18.Server.Models
{
  public class Order
  {
    [Required]
    public int Id { get; set; }
    [Required]
    public int UserId { get; set; }
    [Required]
    public DateTime OrderDate { get; set; }
    [Required]
    public decimal TotalPrice { get; set; }
    [Required]
    public List<OrderDetail> OrderDetails { get; set; }
    [Required]
    public string? FirstName { get; set; }
    [Required]
    public string? LastName { get; set; }
    [Required]
    public string? Street { get; set; }
    [Required]
    public string? Zip { get; set; }
    [Required]
    public string? City { get; set; }
    [Required]
    public string? Country { get; set; }
  }
}
```

LISTING 12-12: Order.cs

```csharp
using System.ComponentModel.DataAnnotations;

namespace eshop_angular_18.Server.Models
{
  public class OrderDTO
  {
    public int Id { get; set; }
    [Required]
    public int UserId { get; set; }
    public DateTime OrderDate { get; set; }
    public decimal TotalPrice { get; set; }
    [Required]
    public List<OrderDetailDTO> OrderDetails { get; set; }
    [Required]
    public CreditCardDTO CreditCard { get; set; }
    [Required]
    public int DeliveryAddressId { get; set; }
    public string? FirstName { get; set; }
    public string? LastName { get; set; }
    public string? Street { get; set; }
    public string? Zip { get; set; }
    public string? City { get; set; }
    public string? Country { get; set; }
  }
}
```

LISTING 12-13: OrderDTO.cs

By comparing the two classes we can see that, for example, the Order class does not contain any credit card details, as we will avoid storing such information in our web app. The two classes also differ in their validation options. When receiving an OrderDTO in our backend, we expect it to contain the user ID, the order details, the delivery address ID selected and the credit card details. The rest of the fields will be used during the controller's response.

On the contrary, the Order class has defined everything as [Required], as we need all this information to be stored in the database.

Let's also see the other classes used:

```csharp
using System.ComponentModel.DataAnnotations;

namespace eshop_angular_18.Server.Models
{
  public class OrderDetail : IValidatableObject
  {
    [Required]
    public int Id { get; set; }
    [Required]
```

```csharp
    public int OrderId { get; set; }
    [Required]
    public int ItemId { get; set; }
    [Required]
    public string? ItemName { get; set; }
    [Required]
    public decimal ItemUnitPrice { get; set; }
    [Required]
    public decimal Quantity { get; set; }
    [Required]
    public decimal TotalPrice { get; set; }

    public IEnumerable<ValidationResult>
      Validate(ValidationContext validationContext)
    {
      if (Quantity <= 0)
      {
        yield return new ValidationResult(
            $"Quantity must be > 0",
            new[] { nameof(Quantity) });
      }
    }
  }
}
```

LISTING 12-14: OrderDetail.cs

```csharp
using System.ComponentModel.DataAnnotations;

namespace eshop_angular_18.Server.Models
{
  public class OrderDetailDTO : IValidatableObject
  {
    public int Id { get; set; }
    public int OrderId { get; set; }
    [Required]
    public int ItemId { get; set; }
    public string? ItemName { get; set; }
    public decimal ItemUnitPrice { get; set; }
    [Required]
    public decimal Quantity { get; set; }
    public decimal TotalPrice { get; set; }

    public IEnumerable<ValidationResult>
      Validate(ValidationContext validationContext)
    {
      if (Quantity <= 0)
      {
        yield return new ValidationResult(
            $"Quantity must be > 0",
            new[] { nameof(Quantity) });
      }
    }
```

```
    }
}
```

LISTING 12-15: OrderDetailDTO.cs

```
using System.ComponentModel.DataAnnotations;

namespace eshop_angular_18.Server.Models
{
  public class CreditCardDTO : IValidatableObject
  {
    [Required]
    public int Id { get; set; }
    [Required]
    [CreditCard]
    public string? CardNumber { get; set; }
    [Required]
    public string? HolderName { get; set; }
    [Required]
    [RegularExpression(@"^[0-9]{3}$", ErrorMessage = "CVV consists of 3 numbers")]
    public string? Code { get; set; }
    [Required]
    [Range(1, 12)]
    public int ExpiryMonth { get; set; }
    [Required]
    [ExpiryYear]
    public int ExpiryYear { get; set; }

    public IEnumerable<ValidationResult>
      Validate(ValidationContext validationContext)
    {
      if (ExpiryYear < DateTime.Now.Year
         || (ExpiryYear == DateTime.Now.Year && ExpiryMonth < DateTime.Now.Month))
      {
        yield return new ValidationResult(
            $"Credit Card has expired",
            new[] { nameof(ExpiryYear) });
      }
    }
  }
}
```

LISTING 12-16: CreditCardDTO.cs

We also have to add another class, `ExpiryYearAttribute`. We will discuss its use later on:

```
using System.ComponentModel.DataAnnotations;

namespace eshop_angular_18.Server.Models
{
```

```
public class ExpiryYearAttribute : ValidationAttribute
{
  protected override ValidationResult?
    IsValid(object? value, ValidationContext validationContext)
  {
    int currentYear = DateTime.Now.Year;
    if (value != null
      && (int)value >= currentYear && (int)value <= currentYear + 4)
    {
      return ValidationResult.Success;
    }

    return new ValidationResult(ErrorMessage
      ?? "Expiration year is out of range ("
        + currentYear + "-" + currentYear + 4 + ")");
  }
}
```

LISTING 12-17: ExpiryYearAttribute.cs

Next, we add the Order entity into EshopContext, so that it can be used by the Entity Framework. Note that we need to specify the exact data type for the decimal fields, like TotalPrice (we choose 2 decimal points):

```
using Microsoft.EntityFrameworkCore;

namespace eshop_angular_18.Server.Models
{
    public class EshopContext : DbContext
    {
        public EshopContext(DbContextOptions<EshopContext> options)
            : base(options)
        {
        }

        public DbSet<Item> Items { get; set; }
        public DbSet<User> Users { get; set; }
        public DbSet<Address> Addresses { get; set; }
        public DbSet<Order> Orders { get; set; }

        protected override void OnModelCreating(ModelBuilder modelBuilder)
        {
            modelBuilder.Entity<Item>().Property(p =>
               p.Price).HasColumnType("decimal(18,2)");
            modelBuilder.Entity<Order>().Property(p
              => p.TotalPrice).HasColumnType("decimal(18,2)");
            modelBuilder.Entity<OrderDetail>().Property(p
              => p.ItemUnitPrice).HasColumnType("decimal(18,2)");
            modelBuilder.Entity<OrderDetail>().Property(p
              => p.Quantity).HasColumnType("decimal(18,2)");
            modelBuilder.Entity<OrderDetail>().Property(p
              => p.TotalPrice).HasColumnType("decimal(18,2)");
```

```
      }
    }
}
```

LISTING 12-18: EshopContext.cs

Finally, we should add a new migration and update the database schema:

```
PM> Add-migration OrderAdded
PM> Update-database
```

Model Validation

With the application up and running, we can now discuss about validation. Although we have used validation in our frontend, it is always important to have the same (and even more) validations in the backend. This happens, because client-side validations can be circumvented, allowing knowledgeable users to attack our backend and database.

In ASP.NET Core, a Web API controller (one that has the [ApiController] annotation) automatically performs validation on receipt of the HTTP request. Here, the OrderDTO validation is performed, as well as the validations of the contained objects, OrderDetailDTO and CreditCard.

Apart from the [Required] validations, in the CreditCardDTO class, we have used the [CreditCard], [RegularExpression] and [Range] annotations. Moreover, we implement the IValidatableObject interface by adding the Validate() method. This method performs the same card expiration check that we saw in the frontend.

The IValidatableObject interface is one way of performing validation, and it is tied to a specific class. If we need a more reusable way, we can create a custom validation attribute by subclassing the ValidationAttribute class (like the ExpiryYearAttribute presented above).

In the ExpiryYearAttribute we perform the validation in the IsValid() method; we check whether the expiration year falls inside the 5-year window (as we did also in the frontend). Then, we apply the [ExpiryYear] attribute to the ExpiryYear property inside CreditCardDTO class.

Finally, in the OrderDetailDTO we check whether the item quantity is higher than zero, or else we return a validation result.

After the DTOs validation, the OrderController builds an Order object based on the OrderDTO object. Note that the frontend sends only the delivery address ID to the backend. The controller then retrieves the address details from the database and stores them in the Order object. We choose to copy a snapshot of the delivery address, in order to avoid the case where this address entry is changed in the future. For the same reason we store also a snapshot of the information about each product, e.g. current price and description, as they may change too.

At this point, and before we store it in the database, we perform validation on the new Order object. We would like to be sure that all required information, such as delivery address and product details, is present in the Order object. If there is a problem with validation we respond with response *400 (Bad Request)*.

After the Order object (and the respective OrderDetails objects) are stored in the database, we create a new OrderDTO object that contains the resulting information, especially the new Order and OrderDetails IDs. This DTO is returned with the *201 (Created)* response.

You may test the submission process with the following dummy Credit Card number:

5555555555554444

In the next chapter, we will deal with error handling.

You may find the code for this chapter here:

https://github.com/htset/eshop-angular-18/tree/part12

13. Error handling and logging

In the previous chapter, we completed the product purchasing process, with the introduction of order validation and submission. One of the shortcomings of the web app, as it stands right now, is the lack of proper error handling and notification. If something goes wrong with the app (e.g. during order submission), the user will not get properly informed of the error. Moreover, the administrator of the app will also not be informed of any problems, as these errors will remain on the client side.

In this chapter, we will implement centralized error handling for our application. Moreover, we will introduce logging functionality on both front- and backend.

Error handling

We choose to implement a centralized solution for error handling, with the combined use of classes that extend the `ErrorHandler` and `HttpInterceptor` classes. The `GlobalErrorHandler` class handles general JavaScript errors and displays a modal dialog box containing the description of the error. It also reports the error to the backend, via the `RemoteLogging` service:

```
import { HttpErrorResponse } from "@angular/common/http";
import { ErrorHandler, Injectable } from "@angular/core";
import { LogMessage } from "../models/logMessage";
import { ErrorDialogService } from "../services/error-dialog.service";
import { LoggingService } from "../services/logging.service";

@Injectable()
export class GlobalErrorHandler implements ErrorHandler {

  constructor(private errorDialogService: ErrorDialogService,
    private remoteLoggingService: LoggingService) { }

  handleError(error: Error | HttpErrorResponse) {
    console.error("Error from global error handler", error);

    let errorMessage = "";
    let stackTrace = "";
    if (error instanceof HttpErrorResponse) {
      errorMessage = "An HTTP error occured. Status: " + error.status
    } else {
      errorMessage = "This operation resulted in an error";
      stackTrace = error.stack || '';
    }

    this.errorDialogService
      .openDialog(errorMessage);

    let logMessage: LogMessage
      = { message: errorMessage, stackTrace: stackTrace };
    this.remoteLoggingService.log(logMessage);
```

    }
}
```

LISTING 13-1: global-error-handler.ts

The `ErrorInterceptor` class intercepts HTTP requests and responses towards the backend and handles any errors pertaining to this interaction. The interceptor is also used to display a loading spinner during the communication with the backend:

```
import { Injectable } from '@angular/core';
import { HttpRequest, HttpHandler, HttpEvent, HttpInterceptor }
  from '@angular/common/http';
import { Observable, throwError } from 'rxjs';
import { catchError, finalize } from 'rxjs/operators';
import { LoadingDialogService } from '../services/loading-dialog.service';
import { AuthenticationService } from '../services/authentication.service';
import { StoreService } from '../services/store.service';

@Injectable()
export class ErrorInterceptor implements HttpInterceptor {

  constructor(private loadingDialogService: LoadingDialogService,
    private authenticationService: AuthenticationService,
    private storeService: StoreService) { }

  intercept(request: HttpRequest<any>, next: HttpHandler)
    : Observable<HttpEvent<any>> {
    const currentUser = this.storeService.user;
    this.loadingDialogService.openDialog();
    return next.handle(request).pipe(
      catchError(error => {
        console.error("Error from error interceptor", error);
        return throwError(() => error);
      }),
      finalize(() => {
        this.loadingDialogService.hideDialog();
      })
    ) as Observable<HttpEvent<any>>;
  }
}
```

LISTING 13-2: error-interceptor.ts

Both classes should be declared in app.module.ts, as `ErrorHandler` and `HTTP_INTERCEPTORS` respectively:

```
...
  providers: [
    provideAnimationsAsync(),
    {
      provide: HTTP_INTERCEPTORS,
```
```

```
      useClass: JwtInterceptor,
      multi: true
    },
    {
      provide: ErrorHandler,
      useClass: GlobalErrorHandler
    },
    {
      provide: HTTP_INTERCEPTORS,
      useClass: ErrorInterceptor,
      multi: true
    }
  ],
  ...
```

LISTING 13-3: app.module.ts

The `ErrorDialog` service uses the `NgbModal` service from Bootstrap for Angular to display a modal dialog box:

```
import { Injectable, Injector } from '@angular/core';
import { NgbModal, NgbModalRef } from '@ng-bootstrap/ng-bootstrap';
import { ErrorDialogComponent } from '../components/shared/error-dialog/error-
dialog.component';

@Injectable({
  providedIn: 'root'
})
export class ErrorDialogService {

  private opened = false;
  private dialogRef?: NgbModalRef;
  private modalService?: NgbModal;

  constructor(private injector: Injector) { }

  openDialog(message: string, info?: string): void {
    if (!this.opened) {
      this.opened = true;
      this.modalService = this.injector.get(NgbModal);
      this.dialogRef = this.modalService.open(ErrorDialogComponent);
      this.dialogRef.componentInstance.message.set(message);
      this.dialogRef.componentInstance.info.set(info);

      this.dialogRef?.closed.subscribe(() => {
        this.opened = false;
      });
    }
  }

  hideDialog() {
    this.dialogRef?.close();
  }
```

}
```

LISTING 13-4: error-dialog.service.ts

We use the `Injector` object to manually inject the `NgbModal` service, because when we try to inject it in the component's constructor, we get a Circular Dependency error.

This dialog box is defined as a component (`ErrorDialogComponent`) that contains two strings:

```
<div class="modal-header">
  <h4 class="modal-title" id="modal-basic-title">Error</h4>
</div>
<div class="modal-body">
  <p class="error-message">
    {{message()}}
  </p>
  @if(info()){
  <p>
    <em>Additional information: {{info()}}</em>
  </p>
  }
</div>
<div class="modal-footer">
  <button type="button" class="btn btn-outline-dark"
          (click)="activeModal.close()">
    Close
  </button>
</div>
```

LISTING 13-5: error-dialog.component.html

We get access to those strings from the outside of the class, with the use of signals:

```
import { Component, OnInit, input, signal } from '@angular/core';
import { NgbActiveModal } from '@ng-bootstrap/ng-bootstrap';

@Component({
  selector: 'app-error-dialog',
  templateUrl: './error-dialog.component.html',
  styleUrls: ['./error-dialog.component.css']
})
export class ErrorDialogComponent implements OnInit {

  message = signal("");
  info = signal("");

  constructor(public activeModal: NgbActiveModal) { }

  ngOnInit(): void {
  }
}
```
```

LISTING 13-6: error-dialog.component.ts

Note: Now that we have the global error handling in place, it is a good idea to remove the localized error handling in the services. For example, we can change the ItemService like this:

...

```
  getItems(page: number, pageSize: number, filter: Filter)
    : Observable<ItemPayload> {
    let categoriesString: string = "";
    filter.categories
      .forEach(cc => categoriesString = categoriesString + cc + "#");
    if (categoriesString.length > 0)
      categoriesString = categoriesString
        .substring(0, categoriesString.length - 1);

    let params = new HttpParams()
      .set("name", filter.name)
      .set("pageNumber", page.toString())
      .set("pageSize", pageSize.toString())
      .set("category", categoriesString);

    return this.http.get<ItemPayload>(this.itemsUrl, { params: params })
      .pipe(
        catchError(this.handleError<ItemPayload>('getItems',
          { items: [], count: 0 }))
      );
  }

  getItem(id: number): Observable<Item> {
    const url = `${this.itemsUrl}/${id}`;
    return this.http.get<Item>(url)
      .pipe(
        catchError(this.handleError<Item>(`getItem/${id}`,
          { id: 0, name: "", price: 0, category: "", description: "" }))
      );
  }
```

...

LISTING 13-7: item.service.ts

In other places, we have chosen to keep error handling locally, e.g. in the Login component:

...

```
  onSubmit() {
    this.submitted = true;

    if (this.loginForm.invalid)
```

```
      return;

    this.loading = true;
    this.authenticationService.login(
      this.loginForm.controls['username'].value,
      this.loginForm.controls['password'].value
    )
    .subscribe({
      next: () => {
        const returnUrl
          = this.route.snapshot.queryParams['returnUrl'] || '/';
        this.router.navigate([returnUrl]);
      },
      error: error => {
        this.error = error.error.message;
        this.loading = false;
      }
    });
  }
...
```

LISTING 13-8: item.service.ts

Loading spinner

We create a loading spinner that will appear to the users as a pop-up dialog. The new component has the following template:

```
<div class="d-flex justify-content-center">
  <div class="spinner-border" role="status"></div>
</div>
```

LISTING 13-9: loading-dialog.component.html

We also have to create a new service (LoadingDialogService) that will handle the opening of the dialog:

```
import { Injectable } from '@angular/core';
import { NgbModal, NgbModalRef } from '@ng-bootstrap/ng-bootstrap';
import {   LoadingDialogComponent   } from   '../components/shared/loading-dialog/loading-dialog.component';

@Injectable({
  providedIn: 'root'
})
export class LoadingDialogService {
  private opened = false;
  private dialogRef?: NgbModalRef;

  constructor(private modalService: NgbModal) { }
```

```
  openDialog(): void {
    if (!this.opened) {
      this.opened = true;
      this.dialogRef = this.modalService.open(LoadingDialogComponent);

      this.dialogRef?.closed.subscribe(() => {
        this.opened = false;
      });
    }
  }

  hideDialog() {
    this.dialogRef?.close();
  }
}
```

LISTING 13-10: loading-dialog.service.ts

Logging

One of the most important features of web application functionality is logging. With logging, we can be informed of how the application is used and of any errors that may happen.

There are some very good logging frameworks available for .NET, such as Serilog, NLog, log4net, and Microsoft.Extensions.Logging library. We opt to go with Serilog in this project, so we will download the following packages from NuGet:

- Serilog: the main package
- Serilog.AspNetCore: support for ASP.NET Core
- Serilog.Enrichers.ClientInfo: enriches the logs with the client's IP and UserAgent information.
- Serilog.Sinks.MSSqlServer: a sink to save logging information to SQL Server

We start with the *Program.cs* file, where we instruct the middleware to use Serilog for logging, we create a new instance of the logger and we enable access to the current HttpContext:

```
var Configuration = builder.Configuration
    .SetBasePath(Directory.GetCurrentDirectory())
    .AddJsonFile("appsettings.json", optional: false, reloadOnChange: true)
    .AddJsonFile($"appsettings.{Environment
            .GetEnvironmentVariable("ASPNETCORE_ENVIRONMENT") ??
                "Production"}.json", optional: true)
    .Build();

Log.Logger = new LoggerConfiguration()
    .ReadFrom.Configuration(Configuration)
    .CreateLogger();
```

```
builder.Host.UseSerilog();

…

builder.Services.AddHttpContextAccessor();

…
```

LISTING 13-11: Program.cs

Finally, we add logging configuration info into *appsettings.json* (and we remove the existing Microsoft.Extensions.Logging configuration):

```
  "Serilog": {
    "MinimumLevel": "Information",
    "WriteTo": [
      {
        "Name": "MSSqlServer",
        "Args": {
          "connectionString":      "Data     Source=localhost\\SQLEXPRESS;Initial
Catalog=angular-eshop-18-DB;Integrated Security=SSPI;Encrypt=False;",
          "tableName": "Logs",
          "autoCreateSqlTable": true
        }
      }
    ],
    "Enrich": [ "WithClientIp", "WithClientAgent" ]
  },
```

LISTING 13-12: appSettings.json

Here, we define the log level (Information) and the SQL Server table where the logging information will be stored (Logs). We also instruct Serilog to add client IP address and UserAgent information into the logs.

The Logs table is created automatically when we run the backend for the first time. The table has the following default structure:

```
CREATE TABLE [dbo].[Logs](
        [Id] [int] IDENTITY(1,1) NOT NULL,
        [Message] [nvarchar](max) NULL,
        [MessageTemplate] [nvarchar](max) NULL,
        [Level] [nvarchar](max) NULL,
        [TimeStamp] [datetime] NULL,
        [Exception] [nvarchar](max) NULL,
        [Properties] [nvarchar](max) NULL
    )
```

LISTING 13-13: SQL code

The properties column contains the additional information that we asked, i.e. IP address and UserAgent info.

Now that we have set up the logging mechanism, we can use it in our project. Remember, errors that happen in the Angular app will be displayed only to the end-user, as we have yet no mechanism to inform ourselves of any problems in the app. For this reason, we create a new Controller (RemoteLoggingController) that will receive error messages from the frontend and will store them in the Logs table:

```
using eshop_angular_18.Server.Models;
using Microsoft.AspNetCore.Http;
using Microsoft.AspNetCore.Mvc;

namespace eshop_angular_18.Server.Controllers
{
  [Route("api/[controller]")]
  [ApiController]
  public class RemoteLoggingController : ControllerBase
  {
    private readonly ILogger Logger;

    public RemoteLoggingController(ILogger<RemoteLoggingController> logger)
      : base()
    {
      Logger = logger;
    }

    [HttpPost]
    public void Post(LogMessage logMessage)
    {
      Logger.LogError("Remote message: {message}, " +
          "Stack trace: {stackTrace}", logMessage.Message,
          logMessage.StackTrace);
    }
  }
}
```

LISTING 13-14: **RemoteLoggingController.cs**

We should also define the LogMessage class:

```
namespace eshop_angular_18.Server.Models
{
  public class LogMessage
  {
    public string? Message { get; set; }
    public string? StackTrace { get; set; }
  }
}
```

LISTING 13-15: **LogMessage.cs**

In the frontend, we create a new Angular service (`LoggingService`) that posts client-side errors to the backend. As we saw earlier, this service is used in the global error handler:

```typescript
import { HttpClient, HttpHeaders } from '@angular/common/http';
import { Injectable } from '@angular/core';
import { environment } from '../../environments/environment';
import { LogMessage } from '../models/logMessage';

@Injectable({
  providedIn: 'root'
})
export class LoggingService {

  httpOptions = {
    headers: new HttpHeaders({ 'Content-Type': 'application/json' })
  };

  constructor(private http: HttpClient) { }

  log(logMessage: LogMessage) {
    this.http.post<LogMessage>(`${environment.apiUrl}/remoteLogging`, logMessage)
        .subscribe();
  }
}
```

LISTING 13-16: logging.service.ts

We also add the `LogMessage` structure:

```typescript
export interface LogMessage {
  message: string,
  stackTrace: string
}
```

LISTING 13-17: logMessage.ts

Bonus stuff: Analytics

Analytics is another valuable source of information for the developers of a web application. With analytics, we can understand how the end-users make use of the application (i.e., which pages they usually visit and which buttons they press).

There are specialized platforms for those operations that can provide us with valuable insights into app usage. We will just use this opportunity to show how we can use Directives to implement cross-cutting features in our code.

We create a new Directive, called `AnalyticsDirective`, inside a new folder (`/src/app/directives`):

```
import { Directive, ElementRef, HostListener, Input } from '@angular/core';
import { Router } from '@angular/router';

@Directive({
  selector: '[appAnalytics]'
})
export class AnalyticsDirective {

  @Input("events") events: string = "";

  constructor(private el: ElementRef,
    private router: Router) { }

  @HostListener('click') onClick() {
    if (this.events.indexOf('click') >= 0) {
      this.logEvent("click");
    }
  }

  @HostListener('change') onInput() {
    if (this.events.indexOf('change') >= 0) {
      this.logEvent("change");
    }
  }

  @HostListener('blur') onBlur() {
    if (this.events.indexOf('blur') >= 0) {
      this.logEvent("blur");
    }
  }

  logEvent(eventName: string) {
    console.log("Event: " + eventName);
    console.log("Element ID: " + this.el.nativeElement.id);
    console.log("Element value: " + this.el.nativeElement.value)
    console.log("Page: " + this.router.url)
  }
}
```

LISTING 13-18: analytics.directive.ts

For the directive to work, we have to apply it to one or more components, by adding the `addAnalytics` selector:

```
  @for(item of storeService.cart.cartItems; track item){
  <tr>

...
    <td>
      <input type="number" [(ngModel)]="item.quantity"
```

```
        size="2" id="quantity"
        appAnalytics events="change blur" />
    </td>
...
    <td>
      <input type="button" (click)="removeFromCart(item)"
        id="remove" value="Remove"
        appAnalytics events="click" />
    </td>
...
<button (click)="emptyCart()" id="empty"
  [disabled]="storeService.cart.cartItems.length == 0"
  appAnalytics events="click">Empty Cart
</button>
</tr>
```

LISTING 13-19: cart.component.html

Here, we apply the directive to the *Remove from Cart* button and the *Quantity* input box on the *Show Cart* page. Next to the `appAnalytics` selector, we add the `events` attribute. This attribute defines the DOM events that the directive should listen to and send to the analytics provider.

The `@HostListener` attribute is the way for the Directive to listen to the HTML element's events. Also, the `ElementRef` object can be used to gain access to the element's attributes, like id and value.

In this simple example, the directive just displays the analytics information on the console log, instead of a specialized platform.

Note: Minor changes were also made in *auth.guard.ts* and *authentication.service.ts*. You can check for them, as well as view the whole code in Github:

https://github.com/htset/eshop-angular-18/tree/part13

14. User registration

In this chapter, we will delve into the details of user registration. We will also see how to help users reset their passwords, when they forget them.

Registration request

First of all, let's create the registration form component:

```
<h2>Registration</h2>
<div class="card">
  <div class="card-body" id="cartBody">
    <form [formGroup]="registrationForm" (ngSubmit)="onSubmit()">
      <div class="form-row">
        <div class="form-group col-md-2">
          <label for="firstName">First Name:</label>
          <input type="text" formControlName="firstName"
                 class="form-control form-control-sm"
                 [ngClass]="{ 'is-invalid': submitted() == true && registrationForm.controls['firstName'].errors }" />
          @if(registrationForm.controls['firstName'].invalid
          && (registrationForm.controls['firstName'].dirty
          || registrationForm.controls['firstName'].touched)){
            <div class="text-danger">
              @if(registrationForm.controls['firstName']
                && registrationForm.controls['firstName'].errors?.['required']){
                <div>
                  First name is required
                </div>
              }
              @if(registrationForm.controls['firstName'].errors?.['minlength']){
                <div>
                  First name must be at least 1 character long
                </div>
              }
            </div>
          }
        </div>
      </div>
      <div class="form-row">
        <div class="form-group col-md-2">
          <label for="lastName">Last Name:</label>
          <input type="text" formControlName="lastName" class="form-control form-control-sm"
                 [ngClass]="{ 'is-invalid': submitted() == true && registrationForm.controls['lastName'].errors }" />
          @if(registrationForm.controls['lastName'].invalid
            && (registrationForm.controls['lastName'].dirty
              || registrationForm.controls['lastName'].touched)){
            <div class="text-danger">
              @if(registrationForm.controls['lastName'].errors?.['required']){
                <div>
                  Last name is required
```

```
            </div>
          }
          @if(registrationForm.controls['lastName'].errors?.['minlength']){
          <div>
            Last name must be at least 1 character long
          </div>
          }
        </div>
        }
      </div>
    </div>
    <div class="form-row">
      <div class="form-group col-md-2">
        <label for="username">User Name:</label>
        <input    type="text"    formControlName="username"    class="form-control form-control-sm"
              [ngClass]="{    'is-invalid':    submitted()    ==    true    &&
registrationForm.controls['username'].errors }" />
          @if(registrationForm.controls['username'].invalid
            && (registrationForm.controls['username'].dirty
              || registrationForm.controls['username'].touched)){
        <div class="text-danger">
          @if(registrationForm.controls['username'].errors?.['required']){
          <div>
            Username is required
          </div>
          }
          @if(registrationForm.controls['username'].errors?.['minlength']){
          <div>
            Username must be at least 4 characters long
          </div>
          }
        </div>
        }
      </div>
    </div>
    <div class="form-row">
      <div class="form-group col-md-2">
        <label for="password">Password:</label>
        <input   type="password"   formControlName="password"   class="form-control form-control-sm"
              [ngClass]="{    'is-invalid':    submitted()    ==    true    &&
registrationForm.controls['password'].errors }" />
          @if(registrationForm.controls['password'].invalid
            && (registrationForm.controls['password'].dirty
              || registrationForm.controls['password'].touched)){
        <div class="text-danger">
          @if(registrationForm.controls['password'].errors?.['required']){
          <div>
            Password is required
          </div>
          }
        </div>
        }
      </div>
    </div>
```

```
    </div>
    <div class="form-row">
      <div class="form-group col-md-2">
        <label for="confirmPassword">Confirm password:</label>
        <input type="password" formControlName="confirmPassword" class="form-control form-control-sm"
               [ngClass]="{ 'is-invalid': submitted() == true && registrationForm.controls['confirmPassword'].errors && registrationForm.errors?.['passwordsMustMatch'] }" />
        @if((registrationForm.controls['confirmPassword'].invalid
            || registrationForm.errors?.['passwordsMustMatch'])
          && (registrationForm.controls['confirmPassword'].dirty
            || registrationForm.controls['confirmPassword'].touched)){
        <div class="text-danger">
          @if(registrationForm.controls['confirmPassword'].errors?.['required']){
          <div>
            Confirm Password is required
          </div>
          }
          @if(registrationForm.errors?.['passwordsMustMatch']){
          <div>
            Passwords must match
          </div>
          }
        </div>
        }
      </div>
    </div>
    <div class="form-row">
      <div class="form-group col-md-2">
        <label for="email">Email:</label>
        <input type="text" formControlName="email" class="form-control form-control-sm"
               [ngClass]="{ 'is-invalid': submitted() == true && registrationForm.controls['email'].errors }" />
        @if(registrationForm.controls['email'].invalid
          && (registrationForm.controls['email'].dirty
            || registrationForm.controls['email'].touched)){
        <div class="text-danger">
          @if(registrationForm.controls['email'].errors?.['required']){
          <div>
            Email is required
          </div>
          }
          @if(registrationForm.controls['email'].errors?.['email']){
          <div>
            Email must be a valid email address
          </div>
          }
        </div>
        }
      </div>
    </div>
    <re-captcha formControlName="recaptcha"
```

```html
                    (resolved)="onCaptchaResolved($event)"
                    siteKey="6LfxP8IfAAAAACCm4xcrhmBi5jL9vKnG4tfoCu2D"></re-
captcha>
      <button type="submit"
              [disabled]="!registrationForm.valid">
        Register
      </button>
    </form>
  </div>

  @if(success() && submitted()){
  <div class="alert alert-success" role="alert">
    Registration was successful. A confirmation email has been sent to:
    {{this.registrationForm.controls.email.value}} <br />
    <button routerLink="/{{this.returnUrl()}}">Continue</button>
  </div>
  }

  @if(!success() && submitted()){
  <div class="alert alert-danger" role="alert">{{errorMessage()}}</div>
  }
</div>
```

LISTING 14-1: registration.component.html

```typescript
import { Component, OnInit, signal } from '@angular/core';
import { FormControl, FormGroup, Validators } from '@angular/forms';
import { ActivatedRoute, Router } from '@angular/router';
import { UserService } from '../../../../app/services/user.service';
import { passwordsMustMatchValidator }
  from '../../../../app/validators/passwordsMustMatch';

@Component({
  selector: 'app-registration',
  templateUrl: './registration.component.html',
  styleUrls: ['./registration.component.css']
})
export class RegistrationComponent implements OnInit {
  submitted = signal<boolean>(false);
  success =signal<boolean>(false);
  errorMessage = signal<string>("");
  returnUrl = signal<string>('/');
  captchaResolved = signal<boolean>(false);

  registrationForm = new FormGroup({
    firstName: new FormControl('',
      [Validators.required, Validators.minLength(1)]),
    lastName: new FormControl('',
      [Validators.required, Validators.minLength(1)]),
    username: new FormControl('',
      [Validators.required, Validators.minLength(4)]),
    password: new FormControl('',
      Validators.required),
```

```
    confirmPassword: new FormControl('',
      Validators.required),
    email: new FormControl('',
      [Validators.required, Validators.email]),
    recaptcha: new FormControl('',
      [Validators.required])
  }, { validators: [passwordsMustMatchValidator] });

  constructor(private userService: UserService,
    public route: ActivatedRoute) { }

  ngOnInit(): void {
  }

  onSubmit() {
    console.warn(this.registrationForm.value);
    this.submitted.set(true);
    if (!this.registrationForm.valid)
      return;

    this.userService.addUser({
      firstName: this.registrationForm.controls['firstName'].value || '',
      lastName: this.registrationForm.controls['lastName'].value || '',
      username: this.registrationForm.controls['username'].value || '',
      password: this.registrationForm.controls['password'].value || '',
      email: this.registrationForm.controls['email'].value || ''
    })
      .subscribe({
        next: () => {
          this.success.set(true);
          this.registrationForm.disable();
          this.returnUrl.set(this.route.snapshot.queryParams['returnUrl']
            || '/');
        },
        error: error => {
          this.success.set(false);
          this.errorMessage = error.error;
        }
      });
  }

  onCaptchaResolved(result: string | null) {
    this.captchaResolved.set((result) ? true : false);
  }
}
```

LISTING 14-2: registration.component.ts

The registration component consists of a reactive form, in the same way as we have seen in previous chapters. However, there is some new stuff that we should talk about.

In addition to per-control validation, this form includes also validation on two controls combined (*password* and *confirmPassword* text boxes). To implement this, we create a validator function in a new folder called `validators`:

```
import {
  AbstractControl, FormGroup,
  ValidationErrors, ValidatorFn
} from "@angular/forms";

export const passwordsMustMatchValidator: ValidatorFn =
  (control: AbstractControl): ValidationErrors | null => {
    const p = control.get('password');
    const rp = control.get('confirmPassword');

    if (rp?.errors) {
      //return if another validator has already
      //found an error on the matchingControl
      return null;
    }
    return p && rp && p.value !== rp.value ?
      { passwordsMustMatch: true } : null;
  }
```

LISTING 14-3: passwordsMustMatch.ts

This validator is used on the `registrationForm` form group as a whole and not on a specific form control. It accesses the contents of both controls and checks if they are equal.

Furthermore, notice that we handle any errors that happen during registration locally, and not through the centralized error control that we introduced in the previous chapter. When we subscribe to the Observable returned from `addUser()` function in `UserService`, we also pass an error handling function that will display the error message on the page and not in a message box. If we omit this function, then the centralized error handling will kick in and will display a message box with the error message.

By the way, function `addUser()` should be defined in `UserService`:

```
...
addUser(user: User) {
  return this.http
    .post<User>(`${environment.apiUrl}/users`, user, this.httpOptions);
}
...
```

LISTING 14-4: user.service.ts

Finally, apart from the usual text controls, the form contains a Recaptcha control, to verify that the requester is not a bot. In order to use the Recaptcha control we have to create a Recaptcha account with Google at https://www.google.com/recaptcha/.

We choose to register a new v2 Racaptcha site and we get a site key that we include in the Recaptcha component (`<re-captcha>`) in the html template. We also implement the `onCaptchaResolved()` callback function that is called upon user verification.

The Recaptcha component is installed with the following:

`npm install ng-recaptcha-2`

We will also have to include the `RecaptchaFormsModule` and `RecaptchaModule` modules in app.module.ts file:

```
import { RecaptchaFormsModule, RecaptchaModule } from 'ng-recaptcha-2';
...
  imports: [
    ...
    RecaptchaModule,
    RecaptchaFormsModule
  ],
...
```

LISTING 15-5: app.module.ts

We will also have to add the `/register` route in app-routing.module.ts file.

On the API side now, we create the Register function that handles calls to /users/register:

```
...
    [HttpPost]
    [AllowAnonymous]
    public async Task<ActionResult<User>> Register([FromBody] User user)
    {
      if (await Context.Users.AnyAsync(u => u.Username == user.Username))
      {
        return BadRequest("Username is already used");
      }

      if (await Context.Users.AnyAsync(u => u.Email == user.Email))
      {
        return BadRequest("Email is already used");
      }

      user.Role = "customer";
      user.Password = PasswordHasher.HashPassword(user.Password);
      user.Status = "Pending";
      user.RegistrationCode = CreateConfirmationToken();

      await Context.Users.AddAsync(user);
      await Context.SaveChangesAsync();

      SendConfirmationEmail(user);

      return CreatedAtAction(nameof(GetUser), new { id = user.Id }, user);
    }
```

```csharp
...
    private string CreateConfirmationToken()
    {
      var randomNum = new byte[64];
      using (var generator = RandomNumberGenerator.Create())
      {
        generator.GetBytes(randomNum);
        var tempString = Convert.ToBase64String(randomNum);
        return tempString.Replace("\\", "")
          .Replace("+", "").Replace("=", "").Replace("/", "");
      }
    }


    private void SendConfirmationEmail(User user)
    {
      var smtpClient = new SmtpClient()
      {
        Host = AppSettings.SmtpHost,
        Port = AppSettings.SmtpPort,
        Credentials = new System.Net.NetworkCredential(AppSettings.SmtpUsername, AppSettings.SmtpPassword),
        EnableSsl = true
      };

      var message = new MailMessage()
      {
        From = new MailAddress("info@my-eshop.com"),
        Subject = "Confirm Registration",
        Body = "To confirm registration please click <a href=\"https://localhost:4200/confirm_registration?code=" + user.RegistrationCode + "\">here</a>",
        IsBodyHtml = true
      };

      message.To.Add(user.Email);

      //smtpClient.Send(message);
    }
...
```

LISTING 14-6: UserController.cs

After we check that the supplied username and the email do not already exist, we create a new user with "Pending" status and we send him an email with a confirmation code.

This code is a randomly generated base64 string, where we replace the \, /, + and = characters that don't play well in URLs. We see that the email body contains a link to the registration confirmation page, in the form of:

```
https://localhost:4200/confirm_registration?code=xxxxxxxx
```

where xxxxxxx is the registration code.

The SMTP server settings have been added to the appsettings.json file:

```
"AppSettings": {
  "Secret": "this is a very long string to be used as secret",
  "SmtpHost": "smtp.host",
  "SmtpPort": 587,
  "SmtpUsername": "username@mysite.com",
  "SmtpPassword": "passssss"
},
```

LISTING 14-7: appSettings.json

We also have to update `AppSettings` class, to reflect this change:

```
namespace eshop_angular_18.Server.Helpers
{
  public class AppSettings
  {
    public string? Secret { get; set; }
    public string? SmtpHost { get; set; }
    public int SmtpPort { get; set; }
    public string? SmtpUsername { get; set; }
    public string? SmtpPassword { get; set; }
  }
}
```

LISTING 14-8: AppSettings.cs

Finally, we also have to add the `Status` and `RegistrationCode` fields into the `User` model:

```
namespace eshop_angular_18.Server.Models
{
  public class User
  {
    public int Id { get; set; }
    public string? FirstName { get; set; }
    public string? LastName { get; set; }
    public string? Username { get; set; }
    public string? Password { get; set; }
    public string? Token { get; set; }
    public string? RefreshToken { get; set; }
    public DateTime? RefreshTokenExpiry { get; set; }
    public string? Role { get; set; }
    public string? Email { get; set; }
    public string? Status { get; set; }
    public string? RegistrationCode { get; set; }
  }
}
```

LISTING 14-9: User.cs

Don't forget to create and apply the necessary migration in the database:

PM> Add-migration Registration

PM> Update-database

Registration confirmation

Next, we create the registration confirmation component. This is where the user will land when he follows the link in the email:

```
<h3>Registration E-mail Confirmation</h3>
<p>{{result}}</p>
<p><button routerLink="/">Go to product list</button></p>
@if(storeService.cart.cartItems.length > 0
  && storeService.cart.isCartValid()){
<p>
  <button routerLink="/cart">Go to cart</button>
</p>
}
```

LISTING 14-10: registration-confirm.component.html

```
import { Component, OnInit } from '@angular/core';
import { ActivatedRoute, Router } from '@angular/router';
import { map, mergeMap, tap } from 'rxjs/operators';
import { StoreService } from '../../../../app/services/store.service';
import { UserService } from '../../../../app/services/user.service';

@Component({
  selector: 'app-registration-confirm',
  templateUrl: './registration-confirm.component.html',
  styleUrls: ['./registration-confirm.component.css']
})
export class RegistrationConfirmComponent implements OnInit {

  result: string = "";

  constructor(
    private route: ActivatedRoute,
    private userService: UserService,
    public storeService: StoreService,
    private router: Router
  ) { }

  ngOnInit(): void {
    let code = '';
    this.route.queryParams.pipe(
```

```
      tap(params => code = params['code']),
      mergeMap(params => this.userService.confirmRegistration(code)),
      map(user => {
        sessionStorage.setItem('user', JSON.stringify(user));
        this.storeService.user = user;
        return user;
      })
    )
      .subscribe({
        next: () => {
          this.result = "Registration was successfully confirmed";
        },
        error: error => {
          this.result = "Registration confirmation failed. " + error.error;
        }
      });
  }
}
```

LISTING 14-11: registration-confirm.component.ts

When the component is loaded, it retrieves the registration code from the query string and calls the `confirmRegistration` function in `UserService`. After the registration has been confirmed, the user is automatically logged in (we set the user object in the session storage).

Note here the use of `mergeMap()` function of RxJS. The process of retrieving the query string is asynchronous. To achieve calling `confirmRegistration()` in sequence, i.e. only after the confirmation code has been retrieved from the query string, we use `pipe()` and `mergeMap()`.

We should also add `confirmRegistration` function in `UserService`:

```
...
confirmRegistration(code: string) {
  return this.http
    .post<User>(`${environment.apiUrl}/users/confirm_registration`,
      { code: code }, this.httpOptions);
}
...
```

LISTING 14-12: user.service.ts

Also, remember to add the `/confirm_registration` route to *app-routing.module.ts* file.

On the API side, here is the respective method called:

```
public class RegistrationCode
{
  public string Code { get; set; }
}
```

```csharp
[Route("api/users")]
[EnableCors("my_eshop_AllowSpecificOrigins")]
[ApiController]
public class UserController : ControllerBase
{

...

    [HttpPost("confirm_registration")]
    [AllowAnonymous]
    public async Task<ActionResult<User>>
        ConfirmRegistration([FromBody] RegistrationCode code)
    {
      var user = await Context.Users
        .SingleOrDefaultAsync(u => u.RegistrationCode == code.Code);
      if (user == null)
      {
        return BadRequest("Registration code not found");
      }

      if (user.Status == "Active")
      {
        return BadRequest("User is already activated");
      }

      user.Status = "Active";
      user.Token = CreateToken(user);
      user.RefreshToken = CreateRefreshToken();
      user.RefreshTokenExpiry = DateTime.Now.AddDays(7);

      await Context.SaveChangesAsync();

      user.Password = null;

      return Ok(user);
    }

...

}
```

LISTING 14-13: UserController.cs

Note here that we define a special purpose class (RegistrationCode) that will be used by ASP.NET Web API to bind and validate the HTTP request payload body and to make it available for us in the method body.

Finally, we have to update our Controller so that users may log in only when they are in the *Active* state:

```csharp
...
    [HttpPost("authenticate")]
    public async Task<IActionResult> Authenticate([FromBody] User formParams)
```

```
{
  if (formParams == null || formParams.Password == null)
    return BadRequest(new { message = "Log in failed" });

  var user = await Context.Users
      .SingleOrDefaultAsync(x => x.Username == formParams.Username);

  if (user == null || user.Password == null)
    return BadRequest(new { message = "Log in failed" });

  if (!PasswordHasher
      .VerifyPassword(formParams.Password, user.Password))
    return BadRequest(new { message = "Log in failed" });

  if (user.Status != "Active")
    return BadRequest(new
    {
      message = "Registration has not been confirmed"
    });

  user.Token = CreateToken(user);
  user.RefreshToken = CreateRefreshToken();
  user.RefreshTokenExpiry = DateTime.Now.AddDays(7);
  Context.SaveChanges();

  user.Password = null;

  return Ok(user);
}
...
```

LISTING 14-14 UserController.cs

Forgot password

This is the component used for the password reset request:

```
<h2>Password Reset</h2>
<div class="card">
  <div class="card-body" id="cartBody">
    <form [formGroup]="forgotForm" (ngSubmit)="onSubmit()">
      <div class="form-row">
        <div class="form-group col-md-2">
          <label for="email">
            Please type your email address:
          </label>
          <input type="text"
                 formControlName="email"
                 class="form-control form-control-sm"
                 [ngClass]="{ 'is-invalid': submitted() == true && forgotForm.controls['email'].errors }" />
          @if(forgotForm.controls['email'].invalid
            && (forgotForm.controls['email'].dirty
```

```
                    || forgotForm.controls['email'].touched)){
                <div class="text-danger">
                  @if(forgotForm.controls['email'].errors?.['required']){
                  <div>
                    Email is required
                  </div>
                  }
                  @if(forgotForm.controls['email'].errors?.['email']){
                  <div>
                    Email must be a valid email address
                  </div>
                  }
                </div>
                }
              </div>
            </div>
            <button type="submit"
                    [disabled]="!forgotForm.valid">
              Submit
            </button>
          </form>
      </div>
      @if(success() && submitted()){
      <div class="alert alert-success" role="alert">
        Password was reset successful.
        An email with instructions has been sent to:
         {{this.forgotForm.controls['email'].value}}
      </div>
      }

      @if(!success() && submitted()){
      <div class="alert alert-danger" role="alert">
         {{errorMessage()}}
      </div>
      }
</div>
```

LISTING 14-15: forgot-password.component.html

```
import { Component, OnInit, signal } from '@angular/core';
import { FormControl, FormGroup, Validators } from '@angular/forms';
import { UserService } from '../../../../app/services/user.service';

@Component({
  selector: 'app-forgot-password',
  templateUrl: './forgot-password.component.html',
  styleUrls: ['./forgot-password.component.css']
})
export class ForgotPasswordComponent implements OnInit {
  submitted = signal<boolean>(false);
  success = signal<boolean>(false);
  errorMessage = signal<string>("");
```

```
  constructor(private userService: UserService) { }

  forgotForm = new FormGroup({
    email: new FormControl('', [Validators.required, Validators.email]),
  });

  ngOnInit(): void {
  }

  onSubmit() {
    console.warn(this.forgotForm.value);
    this.submitted.set(true);

    if (!this.forgotForm.valid)
      return;

    this.userService
      .resetPassword(this.forgotForm.controls['email'].value || '')
      .subscribe({
        next: () => {
          this.success.set(true);

        },
        error: error => {
          this.success.set(false);
          this.errorMessage = error.error;
        }
      });
  }
}
```

LISTING 14-16: forgot-password.component.ts

Here we have a simple reactive form, with only one form control.

We should add `resetPassword` function in `UserService`:

```
...
resetPassword(email: string) {
  return this.http
    .post<User>(`${environment.apiUrl}/users/reset_password`,
      { email: email }, this.httpOptions);
}
...
```

LISTING 14-17: user.service.ts

Don't forget to add the respective routing entry in app-routing.module.ts.

On the API side, we have the `ResetPassword()` method that works similar to registration, i.e. by sending confirmation code via email. Here, we opt to reuse the RegistrationCode field in User object, as well as the `CreateConfirmationToken()` method.

```
public class ResetEmail
{
  public string Email { get; set; }
}

[Route("api/users")]
[EnableCors("my_eshop_AllowSpecificOrigins")]
[ApiController]
public class UserController : ControllerBase
{

...

    [HttpPost("reset_password")]
    [AllowAnonymous]
    public async Task<ActionResult<User>>
      ResetPassword([FromBody] ResetEmail resetEmail)
    {
      var user = await Context.Users
        .SingleOrDefaultAsync(u => u.Email == resetEmail.Email);
      if (user == null)
      {
        return BadRequest("Email not found");
      }

      user.Status = "PasswordReset";
      user.Password = null;
      user.RegistrationCode = CreateConfirmationToken();

      await Context.SaveChangesAsync();

      SendPasswordResetEmail(user);

      return Ok(user);
    }

...

    private void SendPasswordResetEmail(User user)
    {
      var smtpClient = new SmtpClient()
      {
        Host = AppSettings.SmtpHost,
        Port = AppSettings.SmtpPort,
        Credentials = new System.Net
          .NetworkCredential(AppSettings.SmtpUsername, AppSettings.SmtpPassword),
        EnableSsl = true
      };

      var message = new MailMessage()
```

```
    {
       From = new MailAddress("info@my-eshop.com"),
       Subject = "Email reset",
       Body      =     "To     insert     a     new     password,    please     click    <a
href=\"https://localhost:4200/new_password?code="     +     user.RegistrationCode     +
"\">here</a>",
       IsBodyHtml = true
    };

    message.To.Add(user.Email);

    //smtpClient.Send(message);
  }

}
```

LISTING 14-18 UserController.cs

Enter new password

Finally, we create the component that will be used, when the user follows the link in the password reset email:

```
<h2>New Password</h2>
<div class="card">
  <div class="card-body" id="cartBody">

    <form [formGroup]="newPasswordForm" (ngSubmit)="onSubmit()">
      <div class="form-row">
        <div class="form-group col-md-2">
          <label for="password">Password:</label>
          <input type="password"
                 formControlName="password"
                 class="form-control form-control-sm"
                 [ngClass]="{    'is-invalid':    submitted()    ==    true    &&
newPasswordForm.controls['password'].errors }" />
          @if(newPasswordForm.controls['password'].invalid
          && (newPasswordForm.controls['password'].dirty
          || newPasswordForm.controls['password'].touched)){
          <div class="text-danger">
            @if(newPasswordForm.controls['password'].errors?.['required']){
            <div>
              Password is required
            </div>
            }
          </div>
          }
        </div>
      </div>
      <div class="form-row">
        <div class="form-group col-md-2">
          <label for="confirmPassword">Confirm password:</label>
```

```html
            <input type="password"
                formControlName="confirmPassword"
                class="form-control form-control-sm"
                [ngClass]="{ 'is-invalid': submitted() == true &&
newPasswordForm.controls['confirmPassword'].errors &&
newPasswordForm.errors?.['passwordsMustMatch'] }" />
            @if((newPasswordForm.controls['confirmPassword'].invalid
            || newPasswordForm.errors?.['passwordsMustMatch'])
            && (newPasswordForm.controls['confirmPassword'].dirty
            || newPasswordForm.controls['confirmPassword'].touched)){
            <div class="text-danger">

@if(newPasswordForm.controls['confirmPassword'].errors?.['required']){
            <div>
                Confirm Password is required
            </div>
            }
            @if(newPasswordForm.errors?.['passwordsMustMatch']){
            <div>
                Passwords must match
            </div>
            }
            </div>
            }
        </div>
    </div>
    <button type="submit"
        [disabled]="!newPasswordForm.valid">Change password</button>
    </form>
</div>

@if(success() && submitted()){
<div class="alert alert-success" role="alert">
    Password change was successful<br />
    <button routerLink="/login">Log in</button>
</div>
}

@if(!success() && submitted()){
<div class="alert alert-danger" role="alert">
    {{errorMessage()}}
</div>
}
</div>
```

LISTING 14-19: new-password.component.html

```
import { Component, OnInit, signal } from '@angular/core';
import { FormControl, FormGroup, Validators } from '@angular/forms';
import { ActivatedRoute } from '@angular/router';
import { UserService } from '../../../app/services/user.service';
import { passwordsMustMatchValidator } from '../../../app/validators/passwordsMustMatch';
```

```
@Component({
  selector: 'app-new-password',
  templateUrl: './new-password.component.html',
  styleUrls: ['./new-password.component.css']
})
export class NewPasswordComponent implements OnInit {

  submitted = signal<boolean>(false);
  success = signal<boolean>(false);
  errorMessage = signal<string>("");
  emailCode = signal<string>("");

  newPasswordForm = new FormGroup({
    password: new FormControl('', Validators.required),
    confirmPassword: new FormControl('', Validators.required),
  }, { validators: [passwordsMustMatchValidator] });

  constructor(
    private route: ActivatedRoute,
    private userService: UserService) { }

  ngOnInit(): void {
    this.route.queryParams
      .subscribe(params => this.emailCode.set(params['code']));
  }

  onSubmit() {
    this.submitted.set(true);
    if (!this.newPasswordForm.valid)
      return;

    this.userService.changePassword(
      this.newPasswordForm.controls['password'].value || '',
      this.emailCode()
    )
      .subscribe({
        next: () => {
          this.success.set(true);
        },
        error: error => {
          this.success.set(false);
          this.errorMessage = error.error;
        }
      });
  }
}
```

LISTING 14-20: new-password.component.ts

There is not much to see here, just a simple reactive form.

Function changePassword should be added in UserService:

```
...
changePassword(newPassword: string, emailCode: string) {
  return this.http
    .post<User>(`${environment.apiUrl}/users/change_password`,
      { password: newPassword, registrationCode: emailCode },
      this.httpOptions
    );
}
...
```

LISTING 14-21: user.service.ts

On the API side, we have the following method:

```
...
    [HttpPost("change_password")]
    [AllowAnonymous]
    public async Task<ActionResult<User>>
      ChangePassword([FromBody] User inputUser)
    {
      var user = await Context.Users
        .SingleOrDefaultAsync(u =>
          u.RegistrationCode == inputUser.RegistrationCode);

      if (user == null)
      {
        return BadRequest("User not found");
      }

      user.Password = PasswordHasher.HashPassword(inputUser.Password);
      user.Status = "Active";
      user.Token = CreateToken(user);
      user.RefreshToken = CreateRefreshToken();
      user.RefreshTokenExpiry = DateTime.Now.AddDays(7);

      await Context.SaveChangesAsync();

      user.Password = null;

      return Ok(user);
    }
...
```

LISTING 14-22: UserController.cs

Finally, we will add a link to the registration and forgot password pages at the bottom of the login page:

```
...
    <div class="card-body">
      <a routerLink="/register">Register</a> -
      <a routerLink="/forgot_password">Forgot Password</a>
```

```
    </div>
...
```

LISTING 14-22: login.component.html

You may want to update the `status` of the existing users in the `Users` table to `Active`.

You may find the code for this chapter here:

https://github.com/htset/eshop-angular-18/tree/part14

15. Cart in local storage

One important detail with regard to cart functionality is that, when we refresh our page, the cart loses all its contents. That is because the cart is stored in the StoreService object and not in permanent storage (like local storage or database). For this reason, we will store the cart contents into Local Storage, so that it will available even after we close and reopen our browser:

```
import { CartItem } from "./cartItem";

export class Cart {
  cartItems: CartItem[] = [];

  constructor(public cartAsJson: string) {
    if (cartAsJson !== '')
      this.cartItems = JSON.parse(cartAsJson) as CartItem[];
  }

  addItem(cartItem: CartItem) {
    let found: boolean = false;
    this.cartItems = this.cartItems.map(ci => {
      if (ci.item?.id == cartItem.item?.id) {
        ci.quantity++;
        found = true;
      }
      return ci;
    });

    if (!found) {
      this.cartItems.push(cartItem);
    }
    this.updateLocalStorage();
  }

  removeItem(item: CartItem) {
    const index = this.cartItems.indexOf(item, 0);
    if (index > -1) {
      this.cartItems.splice(index, 1);
    }
    this.updateLocalStorage();
  }

  emptyCart() {
    this.cartItems = [];
    this.updateLocalStorage();
  }

  getTotalValue(): number {
    let sum = this.cartItems.reduce(
      (a, b) => { a = a + b.item?.price * b.quantity; return a; }, 0);
    return sum;
  }
```

```
  isCartValid(): boolean {
    if  (this.cartItems.find(cartitem   =>   (cartitem.quantity   ==   null   ||
cartitem.quantity <= 0)) === undefined)
       return true;
    return false;
  }

  updateLocalStorage() {
    console.log(JSON.stringify(this.cartItems))
    localStorage.setItem('cart', JSON.stringify(this.cartItems));
  }
}
```

LISTING 15-1: cart.ts

We also update `StoreService` so that it gets the already stored cart contents on initialization:

```
...
private readonly _cart =
  new BehaviorSubject<Cart>(new Cart(localStorage.getItem('cart') || ''));
readonly cart$ = this._cart.asObservable();

get cart(): Cart {
  return this._cart.getValue();
}

set cart(val: Cart) {
  this._cart.next(val);
}
...
```

LISTING 15-2: store.service.ts

Finally, we have to update `CartComponent` so that local storage is updated when we change the quantity of each product:

```
<h3>Cart Details</h3>
<table class="table table-striped">
  <tr>
    <th> </th>
    <th>Name</th>
    <th>Unit Price</th>
    <th>Quantity</th>
    <th>Total Price</th>
    <th> </th>
  </tr>
  @for(item of storeService.cart.cartItems; track item){
  <tr>
    <td>
      <a routerLink="/items/{{item.item.id}}">
        <img src="/angular.svg" width="70px" />
      </a>
```

```html
      </td>
      <td>
        <a routerLink="/items/{{item.item.id}}">
          {{item.item.name}}
        </a>
      </td>
      <td>
        <a routerLink="/items/{{item.item.id}}">
          {{item.item.price}}
        </a>
      </td>
      <td>
        <input type="number" [(ngModel)]="item.quantity"
               (change)="onQuantityChange($event, item.item.id)"
               size="2" id="quantity"
               appAnalytics events="change blur" />
      </td>
      <td>
        <a routerLink="/items/{{item.item.id}}">
          {{item.item.price * item.quantity}}
        </a>
      </td>
      <td>
        <input type="button" (click)="removeFromCart(item)"
               id="remove" value="Remove"
               appAnalytics events="click" />
      </td>
    </tr>
  }
  <tr>
    <td colspan="4"> </td>
    <td>{{storeService.cart.getTotalValue()}}</td>
    <td> </td>
  </tr>
</table>
<br/>
<br/>
<button (click)="emptyCart()" id="empty"
        [disabled]="storeService.cart.cartItems.length == 0"
        appAnalytics events="click">
  Empty Cart
</button>
<br />
<br />
<button routerLink="/checkout" id="checkout"
        [disabled]="storeService.cart.cartItems.length == 0
                 || !storeService.cart.isCartValid()">
  Go to Checkout..
</button>
<br />
<br/>
<button routerLink="">Back to items</button>
<br />
```

LISTING 15-3: cart.component.html

```typescript
import { Component, OnInit } from "@angular/core";
import { CartItem } from "../../../models/cartItem";
import { StoreService } from "../../../services/store.service";

@Component({
  selector: 'app-cart',
  templateUrl: './cart.component.html',
  styleUrls: ['./cart.component.css']
})
export class CartComponent implements OnInit {

  constructor(public storeService: StoreService) { }

  removeFromCart(item: CartItem) {
    this.storeService.cart.removeItem(item);
  }

  emptyCart() {
    this.storeService.cart.emptyCart();
  }

  ngOnInit(): void {
  }

  onQuantityChange(event: any, itemId: number) {
    let newQuantity = parseInt(event.target.value);
    if (Number.isNaN(newQuantity) || newQuantity < 0) {
      newQuantity = 0;
      event.target.value = 0;
    }

    this.storeService.cart.cartItems =
      this.storeService.cart.cartItems.map(item => {
        if (item.item.id === itemId)
          item.quantity = newQuantity;
        return item;
      });
    this.storeService.cart.updateLocalStorage();
  }
}
```

LISTING 15-4: cart.component.ts

Finally, we must update the Payment Component when it uses the Cart object:

```
...
//Submit order
this.orderService.addOrder(order)
  .subscribe((orderResult: Order) => {
    this.storeService.order = orderResult;
    this.storeService.cart.emptyCart();
    this.storeService.deliveryAddress = -1;
```

```
    this.router.navigate(['/summary']);
  });
...
```

LISTING 15-5: payment.component.ts

You may find the code for this chapter here:

https://github.com/htset/eshop-angular-18/tree/part15

16. Admin functionality

In this chapter, we will enhance the administration part of our site, by adding the necessary functionality for administrators to add, remove and modify products. We will also introduce product image uploading functionality, as well as fix the image source path throughout the project.

Backend

This time we will start with the API. The product images will be stored in a folder (named images) in the backend. To do this, we have to create a new folder, named wwwroot, in our ASP.NET Core project. Inside wwwroot we will create another folder called images. We should also add this folder into *.gitignore* so that the images stored are not tracked by Git.

In *Program.cs* there should be the following line present:

```
app.UseStaticFiles();
```

Next, we define a new model describing the product images:

```
namespace eshop_angular_18.Server.Models
{
  public class Image
  {
    public int Id { get; set; }
    public int ItemId { get; set; }
    public string? FileName { get; set; }
    public string? FileType { get; set; }
  }
}
```

LISTING 16-1: Image.cs

In an effort to make the API as future-proof as possible, we have chosen to create a new class (Image) that will contain information about the image (or images) associated with a specific product. This way, we will be able to make our frontend display more than one image per product in the future, for instance, in an image gallery.

A simpler alternative would be to add the FileName and FileType information directly into the Item class. However, in our case, we choose to add a list of Image objects to the Item object:

```
namespace eshop_angular_18.Server.Models
{
  public class Item
  {
    public int Id { get; set; }
    public string? Name { get; set; }
```

```csharp
    public decimal Price { get; set; }
    public string? Category { get; set; }
    public string? Description { get; set; }
    public List<Image>? Images { get; set; }
  }

}
```

LISTING 16-2: Item.cs

Also, we should add the `Image` model to the DB Context:

```csharp
public DbSet<Image> Images { get; set; }
```

LISTING 16-3: EshopContext.cs

Then we add a new migration and update the database:

```
PM> Add-migration Images

PM> Update-database
```

Next we have to modify the `ItemController` class, in order to add CRUD functionality for our products:

```csharp
using eshop_angular_18.Server.Controllers;
using eshop_angular_18.Server.Models;
using Microsoft.AspNetCore.Authorization;
using Microsoft.AspNetCore.Cors;
using Microsoft.AspNetCore.Mvc;
using Microsoft.EntityFrameworkCore;

namespace eshop_backend.Controllers
{
  [Route("api/items")]
  [EnableCors("angular_eshop_AllowSpecificOrigins")]
  [ApiController]
  public class ItemController : ControllerBase
  {
    private readonly EshopContext _context;

    public ItemController(EshopContext context)
    {
      _context = context;
    }

    [HttpGet]
    public async Task<ActionResult<ItemPayload>> GetItems(
        [FromQuery] QueryStringParameters qsParameters)
    {
      IQueryable<Item> returnItems = _context.Items
```

```csharp
        .Include(it => it.Images)
        .OrderBy(on => on.Id);

    if (qsParameters.Name != null
        && !qsParameters.Name.Trim().Equals(string.Empty))
      returnItems = returnItems
          .Where(item =>
              item.Name.ToLower()
              .Contains(qsParameters.Name.Trim().ToLower()));

    if (qsParameters.Category != null
        && !qsParameters.Category.Trim().Equals(string.Empty))
    {
      string[] categories = qsParameters.Category.Split('#');
      returnItems = returnItems
          .Where(item => categories.Contains(item.Category));
    }

    //get total count before paging
    int count = await returnItems.CountAsync();

    returnItems = returnItems
        .Skip((qsParameters.PageNumber - 1) * qsParameters.PageSize)
        .Take(qsParameters.PageSize);

    List<Item> list = await returnItems.ToListAsync();

    return new ItemPayload(list, count);
}

[HttpGet("{id}")]
public async Task<ActionResult<Item>> GetItem(int id)
{
    var item = await _context.Items
        .Include(it => it.Images)
        .SingleOrDefaultAsync(item => item.Id == id);

    if (item == null)
      return NotFound();

    return Ok(item);
}

[Authorize]
[HttpPost]
public async Task<ActionResult<Item>> PostItem(Item item)
{
    await _context.Items.AddAsync(item);
    await _context.SaveChangesAsync();

    return CreatedAtAction(nameof(GetItem), new { id = item.Id }, item);
}

[Authorize]
[HttpPut("{id}")]
```

```csharp
    public async Task<IActionResult> PutItem(int id, Item item)
    {
      if (id != item.Id)
      {
        return BadRequest();
      }

      _context.Entry(item).State = EntityState.Modified;
      await _context.SaveChangesAsync();

      return NoContent();
    }

    [Authorize]
    [HttpDelete("{id}")]
    public async Task<IActionResult> DeleteItem(int id)
    {
      var item = await _context.Items.FindAsync(id);

      if (item == null)
      {
        return NotFound();
      }

      _context.Items.Remove(item);
      await _context.SaveChangesAsync();

      return NoContent();
    }
  }
}
```

LISTING 16-4: ItemController.cs

We see that we have added the methods for the Add/Edit/Delete functionality. Note that, on deletion of an `Item` object, the corresponding images are also deleted (cascade delete).

Moreover, in the existing two GET methods, we have added the following code:

```
_context.Items.Include(it => it.Images)
```

so that the Entity Framework will eagerly load the corresponding Image objects for each Item. If we fail to add this line, the `items[]` array sent to the frontend will be null.

Frontend

On the Angular side, we start by creating the corresponding model for the image class:

```typescript
export class Image {
  constructor(
    public itemId: number,
    public fileType: string,
    public fileContent: File,
```

```
    public fileName: string
) { }
}
```

LISTING 16-5: image.ts

We also add a list of images in the item model:

```
import { Image } from './image'
export interface Item {
  id: number;
  name: string;
  price: number;
  category: string;
  description?: string;
  images?: Image[];
}
```

LISTING 16-6: item.ts

We proceed with the creation of the `AdminItems` component, which provides a paginated list of all products. This component is very similar to `Items` component, available to all users. However, it provides the ability to add a new product or delete or update an existing one. Moreover, it has the form of a grid instead of the cards-based layout viewed by regular users.

```
Page size:
<select [(ngModel)]="storeService.pageSize"
        (change)="onPageSizeChange()" id="pageSize">
  <option value="3">3</option>
  <option value="5">5</option>
  <option value="10">10</option>
  <option value="50">50</option>
</select>
<br />
<button (click)="openFilter()">Filters</button>
<br/>
<table class="table table-striped">
  <tr>
    <th>ID</th>
    <th>Name</th>
    <th>Unit Price</th>
    <th>Category</th>
  </tr>
  @for(item of storeService.items; track item.id){
  <tr>
    <td>
      <a routerLink="/admin/item/{{item.id}}">
        <img  src="{{imageUrl}}/{{(item.images !== undefined && item.images[0] !== undefined)? item.images[0].fileName : ''}}"
              height="40px" />
```

```html
        </a>
      </td>
      <td>
        <a routerLink="/admin/item/{{item.id}}">
          {{item.name}}
        </a>
      </td>
      <td>
        <a routerLink="/admin/item/{{item.id}}">
          {{item.price}}
        </a>
      </td>
      <td>
        <a routerLink="/admin/item/{{item.id}}">
          {{item.category}}
        </a>
      </td>
      <td><button (click)="delete(item)">Delete</button></td>
    </tr>
    }
</table>

<ngb-pagination [(page)]="storeService.page"
                [pageSize]="storeService.pageSize"
                [collectionSize]="storeService.count"
                (pageChange)="onPageChange($event)">
</ngb-pagination>

<br />
<button routerLink="/admin/new_item">Add new Item</button>
```

LISTING 16-7: admin-items.component.html

```typescript
import { Component, OnInit } from '@angular/core';
import { NgbModal } from '@ng-bootstrap/ng-bootstrap';
import { skip } from 'rxjs/operators';
import { Item } from '../../../../app/models/item';
import { AuthenticationService }
  from '../../../../app/services/authentication.service';
import { ItemService } from '../../../../app/services/item.service';
import { StoreService } from '../../../../app/services/store.service';
import { environment } from '../../../../environments/environment';
import { FilterComponent } from '../../shared/filter/filter.component';

@Component({
  selector: 'app-admin-items',
  templateUrl: './admin-items.component.html',
  styleUrls: ['./admin-items.component.css']
})
export class AdminItemsComponent implements OnInit {

  imageUrl: string = environment.imagesUrl;
```

```typescript
constructor(private itemService: ItemService,
  public storeService: StoreService,
  public authenticationService: AuthenticationService,
  private modalService: NgbModal) { }

getItems(): void {
  this.itemService
    .getItems(this.storeService.page,
      this.storeService.pageSize, this.storeService.filter)
    .subscribe(itemPayload => {
      this.storeService.items = itemPayload.items;
      this.storeService.count = itemPayload.count;
    });
}

delete(item: Item): void {
  this.itemService.deleteItem(item)
    .subscribe(item => {
      this.storeService.page = 1;
      this.getItems();
    });
}

openFilter() {
  this.modalService.open(FilterComponent);
}

onPageChange(newPage: number): void {
  this.storeService.page = newPage;
  this.getItems();
}

onPageSizeChange(): void {
  this.storeService._pageSizeSubject.next(this.storeService.pageSize);
}

ngOnInit(): void {
  this.storeService.pageSizeChanges$
    .subscribe(newPageSize => {
      console.log('new page size:' + this.storeService.pageSize);
      this.storeService.page = 1;
      this.getItems();
    });

  this.storeService.filter$
    .pipe(skip(1))    //skip getting filter at component creation
    .subscribe(newFilter => {
      this.storeService.page = 1;
      this.getItems();
    });

  this.getItems();
  }
}
```

LISTING 16-8: admin-items.component.ts

We proceed with updating the `ItemService`, so that it provides functions for inserting new items as well as updating and deleting existing ones:

```
import { Injectable, } from '@angular/core';
import { Observable, catchError, of } from 'rxjs';
import { Item } from '../models/item';
import { ItemPayload } from '../models/itemPayload';
import { Filter } from '../models/filter';
import { HttpClient, HttpHeaders, HttpParams } from '@angular/common/http';
import { environment } from '../../environments/environment';

@Injectable({
  providedIn: 'root'
})
export class ItemService {

  itemsUrl = `${environment.apiUrl}/items`;

  httpOptions = {
    headers: new HttpHeaders({ 'Content-Type': 'application/json' })
  };

  getItems(page: number, pageSize: number, filter: Filter)
    : Observable<ItemPayload> {
    let categoriesString: string = "";
    filter.categories
      .forEach(cc => categoriesString = categoriesString + cc + "#");
    if (categoriesString.length > 0)
      categoriesString = categoriesString
        .substring(0, categoriesString.length - 1);

    let params = new HttpParams()
      .set("name", filter.name)
      .set("pageNumber", page.toString())
      .set("pageSize", pageSize.toString())
      .set("category", categoriesString);

    return this.http.get<ItemPayload>(this.itemsUrl, { params: params });
  }

  getItem(id: number): Observable<Item> {
    const url = `${this.itemsUrl}/${id}`;
    return this.http.get<Item>(url);
  }

  updateItem(item: Item): Observable<Item> {
    const id = item.id;
    const url = `${this.itemsUrl}/${id}`;

    return this.http.put<Item>(url, item, this.httpOptions);
  }
```

```
  addItem(item: Item): Observable<Item> {
    return this.http.post<Item>(this.itemsUrl, item, this.httpOptions);
  }

  deleteItem(item: Item | number): Observable<Item> {
    const id = typeof item === 'number' ? item : item.id;
    const url = `${this.itemsUrl}/${id}`;

    return this.http.delete<Item>(url, this.httpOptions);
  }

  constructor(private http: HttpClient) { }
}
```

LISTING 16-9: item.service.ts

Then, we proceed by creating the AdminItemForm component. This component will be used by admins to edit the details of a product, as well as upload a new image for the product. Adding a new product is a two-step process; first we create and save the new product, then we upload its picture.

Note that, for educational purposes, this time we choose to create a template-driven form, instead of a reactive one:

```
<div class="container">
  <div style="width:50%;float:left;">
    <h3>{{item().name}}</h3>
    <form (ngSubmit)="onSubmit()" #itemForm="ngForm">
      <div class="form-group col-md-4">
        <label for="id">ID</label>
        <input type="text" class="form-control form-control-sm"
               id="id"
               readonly
               [(ngModel)]="item().id"
               name="id"
               #id="ngModel">
      </div>

      <div class="form-group col-md-8">
        <label for="name">Name</label>
        <input type="text" class="form-control form-control-sm"
               id="name"
               required
               [(ngModel)]="item().name"
               name="name"
               #name="ngModel">

        @if(name.invalid && (name.dirty || name.touched)){
          <div class="alert alert-danger">Name is required</div>
        }
      </div>
```

```html
    <div class="form-group col-md-4">
      <label for="price">Price</label>
      <input type="text" class="form-control form-control-sm"
             id="price"
             required
             [ngClass]="{ 'is-invalid':  item().price <= 0 }"
             [(ngModel)]="item().price" name="price"
             #price="ngModel">

      @if(price.invalid && (price.dirty || price.touched)){
      <div class="alert alert-danger">Price is required</div>
      }
      @if(price.value <= 0 && (price.dirty || price.touched)){
      <div class="alert alert-danger">Price must be greater than zero</div>
      }
    </div>

    <div class="form-group col-md-8">
      <label for="description">Description</label>
      <textarea class="form-control form-control-sm"
             id="description"
             [(ngModel)]="item().description"
             name="description">
        </textarea>
    </div>

    <div class="form-group col-md-8">
      <label for="category">Item category</label>
      <select class="form-control form-control-sm"
             id="category"
             required
             [(ngModel)]="item().category" name="category"
             #category="ngModel">
        @for(cat of categories; track cat){
        <option [value]="cat">{{cat}}</option>
        }
      </select>
      @if(category.invalid && (category.dirty || category.touched)){
      <div class="alert alert-danger">Category is required</div>
      }
    </div>

    <div class="form-group col-md-8">
      <button type="submit" id="submit"
             [disabled]="!itemForm.form.valid || itemForm.form.pristine">
        Save
      </button>
      <button type="button" id="back" (click)="goBack()">Back</button>
    </div>
</form>

@if(success() && submitted()){
<div class="alert alert-success"
     role="alert">Item was saved</div>
```

```
      }
      @if(!success() && submitted()){
      <div class="alert alert-danger"
            role="alert">Item was not saved</div>
      }

    </div>

    @if(item().id > 0){
    <div style="width:50%; float:left;vertical-align: middle;">
      <img [src]="imageLink()" alt="product image" style="border-style: solid;" />
      <div class="row" style="margin-bottom:15px;">
        <div class="col-md-3">
          <input #imageInput type="file" #file placeholder="Choose file"
                  (change)="processFile(imageInput)" style="display:none;">
          <button type="button" class="btn btn-success"
                  (click)="file.click()">
            Upload File
          </button>
        </div>
        <div class="col-md-4">
          <span class="upload" *ngIf="progress() > 0">
            {{progress()}}%
          </span>
          <span class="upload" *ngIf="message()">
            {{message()}}
          </span>
        </div>
      </div>
    </div>
    }
</div>
```

LISTING 16-10: admin-item-form.component.html

```
import { Component, OnInit, ViewChild, signal } from '@angular/core';
import { NgForm } from '@angular/forms';
import { ActivatedRoute, Router } from '@angular/router';
import { Item } from '../../../../app/models/item';
import { ItemService } from '../../../../app/services/item.service';
import { Location } from '@angular/common';
import { HttpEventType } from '@angular/common/http';
import { environment } from '../../../../environments/environment';
import { ImageService } from '../../../../app/services/image.service';
import { Image } from '../../../../app/models/image';


@Component({
  selector: 'app-admin-item-form',
  templateUrl: './admin-item-form.component.html',
  styleUrls: ['./admin-item-form.component.css']
})
export class AdminItemFormComponent implements OnInit {
```

```typescript
  @ViewChild('itemForm') public itemForm?: NgForm;
  categories: string[] = ["", "Shoes", "Clothes", "Glasses"];
  mode = signal<string>("new");
  item = signal<Item>({ id: 0, name: "", price: 0, category: "", description: ""
});
  public progress = signal<number>(0);
  public message = signal<string>('');
  success = signal<boolean>(false);
  submitted = signal<boolean>(false);
  imageLink = signal<string>('');
  image?: Image;

  constructor(
    private route: ActivatedRoute,
    public itemService: ItemService,
    private location: Location,
    private router: Router,
    private imageService: ImageService
  ) { }

  ngOnInit(): void {
    this.getItem();
  }

  onSubmit(): void {
    if (this.item().id > 0) {
      this.itemService.updateItem(this.item())
        .subscribe({
          next: () => {
            this.itemForm?.form.markAsPristine();
            this.success.set(true);
            this.submitted.set(true);
          },
          error: () => {
            this.success.set(false);
            this.submitted.set(true);
          }
        });
    }
    else {
      this.itemService.addItem(this.item())
        .subscribe((item) => {
          this.item.set(item);
          this.itemForm?.form.markAsPristine();
        });
    }
  }

  getItem(): void {
    if (this.route.snapshot.paramMap.get('id') === 'undefined'
      || this.route.snapshot.paramMap.get('id') === null
      || Number(this.route.snapshot.paramMap.get('id')) === 0) {

      this.item.set({ id: 0, name: "", price: 0, category: "",
```

```
        description: "" });
    }
    else {
      const id = Number(this.route.snapshot.paramMap.get('id'));
      if (id > 0) {
        this.itemService.getItem(id)
          .subscribe((item) => {
            this.item.set(item);
            let imagesArray = this.item()?.images;
            if (imagesArray !== undefined)
              this.imageLink.set(`${environment.imagesUrl}/`
                + imagesArray[0]?.fileName + '?' + Math.random());
          });
      }
      else {
        this.router.navigate(['/404']);
      }
    }
  }

  goBack(): void {
    this.location.back();
  }

  processFile(imageInput: any) {
    const file: File = imageInput.files[0];
    const reader = new FileReader();

    reader.addEventListener('load', (event: any) => {
      let fileExtension = file.name.split('?')[0].split('.').pop();
      this.image = new Image(this.item().id,
        file.type, file, this.item().id.toString() + '.' + fileExtension);

      this.imageService.upload(this.image)
        .subscribe(event => {
          if (event.type === HttpEventType.UploadProgress)
            this.progress.set(Math
              .round(100 * event.loaded / (event.total || 1)));
          else if (event.type === HttpEventType.Response) {
            this.message.set('Upload success.');
            this.updateImageLink();
          }
        });
    });
    reader.readAsDataURL(file);
  }

  public updateImageLink() {
    this.imageLink.set(`${environment.imagesUrl}/`
      + this.image?.fileName + '?' + Math.random());
  }
}
```

LISTING 16-11: admin-item-form.component.ts

When the user chooses to add a new image for this item, the `processFile()` function is called. This function creates a new `Image` object that contains the actual image, along with image file information and sends it to the backend via the `ImageService`. Tha same function also shows the progress of the uploading as a percentage.

Here is the code for the `ImageService`:

```typescript
import { HttpClient, HttpEvent } from '@angular/common/http';
import { Injectable } from '@angular/core';
import { Observable } from 'rxjs';
import { environment } from '../../environments/environment';
import { Image } from '../../app/models/image';

@Injectable({
  providedIn: 'root'
})
export class ImageService {

  constructor(private http: HttpClient) { }

  public upload(image: Image): Observable<HttpEvent<Response>> {
    const formData = new FormData();

    formData.append('image', image.fileContent, image.fileName);
    formData.append('id', image.itemId.toString());
    return this.http.post<Response>(`${environment.apiUrl}/image`,
      formData, { reportProgress: true, observe: 'events' });
  }

  public getImage(itemId: number): Observable<Image> {
    return this.http.get<Image>(`${environment.apiUrl}/image/${itemId}`);
  }
}
```

LISTING 16-12: image.service.ts

The `ImageService` calls the `` `${environment.apiUrl}/image` `` URL in the backend. We will create the respective controller later in this chapter.

Let's not forget to add the routing entries:

```typescript
...
  {
    path: 'admin', component: AdminHomeComponent,
    canActivate: [AuthGuard],
    children: [
      {
        path: 'users',
        component: AdminUsersComponent,
        canActivate: [AuthGuard]
      },
```

```
    {
      path: 'items',
      component: AdminItemsComponent,
      canActivate: [AuthGuard]
    },
    {
      path: 'item/:id',
      component: AdminItemFormComponent,
      canActivate: [AuthGuard]
    },
    {
      path: 'new_item',
      component: AdminItemFormComponent,
      canActivate: [AuthGuard]
    }
  ]
},
...
```

LISTING 16-13: app-routing.module.ts

The routes are children of the admin route; for example the items route will be called as admin/users.

We also add the link to the admin version of item catalog:

```
<h2>Admin pages</h2>
<nav class="navbar navbar-expand-lg navbar-light bg-light">
  <div class="container-fluid">
    <ul class="navbar-nav">
      <li class="nav-item">
        <a class="nav-link"
           routerLink="/admin/users">Users </a>
      </li>
      <li class="nav-item">
        <a class="nav-link"
           routerLink="/admin/items">Items </a>
      </li>
    </ul>
  </div>
</nav>
<router-outlet></router-outlet>
```

LISTING 16-14: admin-home.component.html

Finally, we should add the URL for the images folder in the environments files:

```
export const environment = {
  production: false,
  apiUrl: 'https://localhost:7141/api',
  imagesUrl: 'https://localhost:7141/images'
};
```

LISTING 16-15: environment.development.ts

```
export const environment = {
  production: true,
  apiUrl: 'https://localhost:7141/api',
  imagesUrl: 'https://localhost:7141/images'
};
```

LISTING 16-16: environment.ts

Backend (again)

Now, we return to backend in order to create the controller for the `${environment.apiUrl}/image` URL:

```
using eshop_angular_18.Server.Models;
using Microsoft.AspNetCore.Cors;
using Microsoft.AspNetCore.Mvc;
using Microsoft.EntityFrameworkCore;
using System.Net.Http.Headers;

namespace eshop_backend.Controllers
{
  [Route("api/[controller]")]
  [EnableCors("angular_eshop_AllowSpecificOrigins")]
  [ApiController]
  public class ImageController : ControllerBase
  {
    private readonly EshopContext Context;

    public ImageController(EshopContext context)
    {
      Context = context;
    }

    [HttpPost, DisableRequestSizeLimit]
    public async Task<ActionResult> UploadImage()
    {
      try
      {
        var formCollection = await Request.ReadFormAsync();
        var file = formCollection.Files.First();

        var folderName = Path.Combine("wwwroot", "images");
        var pathToSave
          = Path.Combine(Directory.GetCurrentDirectory(), folderName);

        if (file.Length > 0)
        {
          var fileName = ContentDispositionHeaderValue
```

```
                .Parse(file.ContentDisposition).FileName?.Trim('"');
            var fullPath = Path.Combine(pathToSave, fileName);
            var dbPath = Path.Combine(folderName, fileName);

            using (var stream = new FileStream(fullPath, FileMode.Create))
            {
              file.CopyTo(stream);
            }

            var itemId = int.Parse(fileName.Substring(0, fileName.IndexOf('.')));
            var fileType = fileName
                .Substring(fileName.IndexOf('.') + 1,
                    fileName.Length - fileName.IndexOf('.') - 1);
            var image = await Context.Images
                .FirstOrDefaultAsync(img => img.ItemId == itemId);
            if (image == null)
            {
              image = new Image()
              {
                ItemId = itemId,
                FileName = fileName,
                FileType = fileType
              };
              await Context.Images.AddAsync(image);
            }
            else
            {
              image.FileName = fileName;
              image.FileType = fileType;
            }

            await Context.SaveChangesAsync();

            return Ok(new { dbPath });
          }
          else
          {
            return BadRequest();
          }
        }
        catch (Exception ex)
        {
          return StatusCode(500, $"Internal server error: {ex}");
        }
      }
    }
  }
}
```

LISTING 16-17: ImagesController.cs

One more thing...

Now that we have a new place to get the images from, we should update the respective components that display the items list and the item details to the customers (i.e. `ItemsComponent` and `ItemsDetailsComponent` classes). The code is almost the same as the one we used for the Admin components and you can find it in the GitHub repository below:

https://github.com/htset/eshop-angular-18/tree/part16

17. Order processing

In this chapter we will complete the web store functionality, by creating the admin pages needed for order processing.

Backend

Instead of providing a RESTful endpoint, as we did for the items list, here we will use OData. OData is a standard supported by Microsoft that defines a set of best practices for building and consuming RESTful APIs.

First of all, we have to install the `Microsoft.AspNetcore.OData` package from NuGet. At the time of writing, the version installed was 8.2.25.

Then, we proceed with adding GET functionality in the `OrderController`:

```
using eshop_angular_18.Server.Models;
using Microsoft.AspNetCore.Mvc;
using Microsoft.AspNetCore.OData.Query;
using Microsoft.EntityFrameworkCore;

namespace eshop_angular_18.Server.Controllers
{
  [Route("api/[controller]")]
  [ApiController]
  public class OrderController : ControllerBase
  {
    private readonly EshopContext _context;

    public OrderController(EshopContext context)
    {
      _context = context;
    }

    [EnableQuery]
    [HttpGet]
    public IQueryable<Order> GetOrders()
    {
      return this._context.Orders
          .AsQueryable();
    }

    [HttpGet("{id}")]
    public async Task<ActionResult<Item>> GetOrder(int id)
    {
      var order = await this._context
          .Orders
          .Include(o => o.OrderDetails)
          .Where(o => o.Id == id)
          .FirstOrDefaultAsync();
      return Ok(order);
    }
```

```
...
}
```

LISTING 17-1: OrderController.cs

Note that we had to change the name of the class from OrderController to OrdersController, as it seemed to create problems with OData.

Furthermore, we have added two methods:

- GetOrders() for retrieving all orders
- GetOrder() to get an order by its ID

The important stuff here is GetOrders() as we have done two things:

- We have annotated this method with the [EnableQuery] attribute
- The method returns an IQueryable reference to the Orders EF entity

By using IQueryable, OData will be able to query the entity in various ways, as we will see next.

We also have to configure OData in *Program.cs*:

```
...
static IEdmModel GetEdmModel()
{
    var obuilder = new ODataConventionModelBuilder();
    obuilder.EntitySet<Order>("Orders");
    obuilder.EnableLowerCamelCase();
    return obuilder.GetEdmModel();
}
...

builder.Services.AddControllers()
    .AddOData(options => options
        .AddRouteComponents("odata", GetEdmModel())
        .Select()
        .Filter()
        .OrderBy()
        .SetMaxTop(50)
        .Count());
...
```

LISTING 17-2: Program.cs

With AddOData we create an OData endpoint that will:

- contain "odata" in the URL (instead of "api")
- enable selection, filtering, ordering, count, etc.
- bring up to 50 entries at each call

Now, we can run our API and we can send some OData requests, like:

/odata/orders?$top=5	Get top 5 entries
/odata/orders?$count=true	Get total entry count (along with the entries)
/odata/orders?$filter=city eq 'New York'	Get entries where city='New York'
/odata/orders?$filter=contains(city,%20%27York%27)	Get entries where city contains 'York'
/odata/orders?$orderby=totalPrice	Order entries by totalPrice
/odata/orders?$skip=5	Skip 5 first entries and return the rest

Those parameters can be combined in order to make more refined queries, i.e:

/odata/orders?$top=5&$skip=5&$count=true&$filter=city eq 'New York'

Frontend

We start by creating the component that displays all submitted orders.

```
Page size:
<select [(ngModel)]="storeService.orderPageSize"
        (change)="onPageSizeChange()" id="pageSize">
  <option value="3">3</option>
  <option value="5">5</option>
  <option value="10">10</option>
  <option value="50">50</option>
</select>
<br />
Search:
<input type="text" [(ngModel)]="search"
       (keyup)="onSearchChange($event)" />
<br />
<table class="table table-striped">
  <tr>
    <th>ID</th>
    <th>Name</th>
    <th>City</th>
    <th>Date</th>
    <th>Price</th>
  </tr>

  @for(order of storeService.orders; track order){
  <tr>
    <td>
      <a routerLink="/admin/order/{{order.id}}">
        {{order.id}}
      </a>
    </td>
```

```html
      <td>
        <a routerLink="/admin/order/{{order.id}}">
          {{order.firstName + ' ' + order.lastName}}
        </a>
      </td>
      <td>
        <a routerLink="/admin/order/{{order.id}}">
          {{order.city}}
        </a>
      </td>
      <td>
        <a routerLink="/admin/order/{{order.id}}">
          {{order.orderDate | date:'short':'IST'}}
        </a>
      </td>
      <td>
        <a routerLink="/admin/order/{{order.id}}">
          {{order.totalPrice}}
        </a>
      </td>
    </tr>
    }
</table>

<ngb-pagination [(page)]="storeService.orderPage"
                [pageSize]="storeService.orderPageSize"
                [collectionSize]="storeService.orderCount"
                (pageChange)="onPageChange($event)">
</ngb-pagination>
```

LISTING 17-3: admin-orders.component.html

```typescript
import { Component, OnInit } from '@angular/core';
import { AuthenticationService } from '../../../services/authentication.service';
import { OrderService } from '../../../services/order.service';
import { StoreService } from '../../../services/store.service';

@Component({
  selector: 'app-admin-orders',
  templateUrl: './admin-orders.component.html',
  styleUrls: ['./admin-orders.component.css']
})
export class AdminOrdersComponent implements OnInit {

  search: string = "";

  constructor(private orderService: OrderService,
    public storeService: StoreService,
    public authenticationService: AuthenticationService) { }

  getOrders(): void {
    this.orderService
```

```
      .getOrders(this.storeService.orderPage,
        this.storeService.orderPageSize, this.search)
      .subscribe(orders => {
        this.storeService.orders = orders.value;
        this.storeService.orderCount = orders["@odata.count"];
      });
  }

  onPageChange(newPage: number): void {
    this.storeService.orderPage = newPage;
    this.getOrders();
  }

  onPageSizeChange(): void {
    this.storeService._orderPageSizeSubject
      .next(this.storeService.orderPageSize);
  }

  ngOnInit(): void {
    this.storeService.orderPageSizeChanges$
      .subscribe(newPageSize => {
        this.storeService.orderPage = 1;
        this.getOrders();
      });

    this.getOrders();
  }

  onSearchChange(event: any) {
    this.getOrders();
  }
}
```

LISTING 17-4: admin-orders.component.ts

This component also enables admin users to search orders with regard to first name, last name and city, by using the search text input.

Next, we create another component that will display detailed information about each order:

```
<h3>{{order.firstName + ' ' + order.lastName}}</h3>
<div>
  <div class="row">
    <div class="col-md-6">Order Date: {{order.orderDate | date:'short':'IST'}}</div>
  </div>
  <div class="row">
    <div class="col-md-6">Total Price: {{order.totalPrice}}</div>
  </div>
  <div class="row">
    <div class="col-md-6">Address: {{order.street + ',' + order.zip + ' ' +
```

```
              order.city + ', ' + order.country}}</div>
            </div>
          </div>
          <div>
            <table class="table">
              <thead>
                <tr>
                  <th>Item Name</th>
                  <th>Quantity</th>
                  <th>Unit Price</th>
                  <th>Total Price</th>
                </tr>
              </thead>
              <tbody>
                @for(details of order.orderDetails; track details){
                  <tr>
                    <td>
                      {{details.itemName}}
                    </td>
                    <td>
                      {{details.quantity}}
                    </td>
                    <td>
                      {{details.itemUnitPrice}}
                    </td>
                    <td>
                      {{details.totalPrice}}
                    </td>
                  </tr>
                }
              </tbody>
            </table>
          </div>
          <div class="row">
            <div class="col-md-3">
              <button routerLink="/admin/orders">Back to orders</button>
            </div>
          </div>
```
LISTING 17-5: admin-order-details.component.html

```
import { Component, OnInit } from '@angular/core';
import { ActivatedRoute } from '@angular/router';
import { Order } from '../../../../app/models/order';
import { OrderService } from '../../../services/order.service';

@Component({
  selector: 'app-admin-order-details',
  templateUrl: './admin-order-details.component.html',
  styleUrls: ['./admin-order-details.component.css']
})
export class AdminOrderDetailsComponent implements OnInit {
```

```
  order: Order = { id: 0 };

  constructor(private route: ActivatedRoute,
    private orderService: OrderService) { }

  getOrder(): void {
    const id = Number(this.route.snapshot.paramMap.get('id'));
    this.orderService
      .getOrder(id)
      .subscribe(order => {
        this.order = order;
      });
  }

  ngOnInit(): void {
    this.getOrder();
  }
}
```

LISTING 17-6: admin-order-details.component.ts

Both components make use of the `OrderService`:

```
import { HttpClient, HttpHeaders, HttpParams } from '@angular/common/http';
import { Injectable } from '@angular/core';
import { Observable } from 'rxjs';
import { environment } from '../../environments/environment';
import { Order } from '../models/order';

@Injectable({
  providedIn: 'root'
})
export class OrderService {

  httpOptions = {
    headers: new HttpHeaders({ 'Content-Type': 'application/json' })
  };
  constructor(private http: HttpClient) { }

  addOrder(order: Order) {
    return this.http
      .post<Order>(`${environment.apiUrl}/orders`, order);
  }

  getOrders(page: number, pageSize: number, search: string)
    : Observable<any> {

    let params = new HttpParams();

    if (page > 1)
      params = params.set("$skip", ((page - 1) * pageSize).toString())
```

```
    params = params.set("$count", "true")
    params = params.set("$top", pageSize.toString());

    if (search != "")
      params = params.set("$filter", "contains(firstName,'" + search
        + "') or contains(lastName,'" + search
        + "') or contains(city,'" + search + "')");

    return this.http
      .get<any>(`${environment.oDataUrl}/orders`, { params: params })
  }

  getOrder(orderId: number): Observable<Order> {
    return this.http
      .get<Order>(`${environment.apiUrl}/orders/${orderId}`);
  }
}
```
LISTING 17-7: order.service.ts

We see here that in `getOrders` function we use the `params` map to create the OData query string. By using `$top` and `$skip` we can enable pagination, while with `$filter` we can select the desired entries. Finally, we use `$count` to get the total count of all order entries (before the `$filter` is applied) so that we can provide it to the pagination component.

Since this pagination component is separate from the one in the items list component, we have to define its own variables in `StoreService`:

```
...
private readonly _orders = new BehaviorSubject<Order[]>([]);
readonly orders$ = this._orders.asObservable();

get orders(): Order[] {
return this._orders.getValue();
}

set orders(val: Order[]) {
this._orders.next(val);
}

private readonly _orderPage = new BehaviorSubject<number>(1);
readonly orderPage$ = this._orderPage.asObservable();

get orderPage(): number {
return this._orderPage.getValue();
}

set orderPage(val: number) {
this._orderPage.next(val);
}

public orderPageSize: number = 3;
public readonly _orderPageSizeSubject = new Subject<number>();
```

```typescript
public orderPageSizeChanges$ = this._orderPageSizeSubject.asObservable();

private readonly _orderCount = new BehaviorSubject<number>(1);
readonly orderCount$ = this._orderCount.asObservable();

get orderCount(): number {
return this._orderCount.getValue();
}

set orderCount(val: number) {
this._orderCount.next(val);
}
...
```

LISTING 17-8: store.service.ts

Let's not forget to add the routing entries:

```typescript
...
{
  path: 'orders',
  component: AdminOrdersComponent,
  canActivate: [AuthGuard]
},
{
  path: 'order/:id',
  component: AdminOrderDetailsComponent,
  canActivate: [AuthGuard]
}
...
```

LISTING 17-9: app-routing.module.ts

Also, we add a new menu entry at admin home:

```html
<h2>Admin pages</h2>
<nav class="navbar navbar-expand-lg navbar-light bg-light">
  <div class="container-fluid">
    <ul class="navbar-nav">
      <li class="nav-item">
        <a class="nav-link"
           routerLink="/admin/users">Users </a>
      </li>
      <li class="nav-item">
        <a class="nav-link"
           routerLink="/admin/items">Items </a>
      </li>
      <li class="nav-item">
        <a class="nav-link"
           routerLink="/admin/orders">Orders </a>
      </li>
    </ul>
```

```
    </div>
</nav>
<router-outlet></router-outlet>
```

LISTING 17-10: admin-home.component.html

Finally, we add the OData specific URL and we are good to go:

```
export const environment = {
  production: false,
  apiUrl: 'https://localhost:7141/api',
  oDataUrl: 'https://localhost:7141/odata',
  imagesUrl: 'https://localhost:7141/images'
};
```

LISTING 17-11: environment.development.ts

There are many things we could do with order processing, like editing the order details, toggling the order's state, and so on. This is left as exercise to the reader.

You may find the code for this chapter in GitHub:

https://github.com/htset/eshop-angular-18/tree/part18

18. Angular testing – part 1

In this chapter, we will introduce unit testing capabilities to our web application. Unit testing is essential during development, as it make us fell more assured that our app works as expected.

We will start by running all the tests that have been automatically generated by the Angular CLI, when we created the components and the services of our web site:

```
ng test
```

We will see that almost all tests fail. That's because in the components and the services that we have written so far, we have made extensive use of the `HttpClient` and `Router` modules. When we create the testbed to run our unit tests, we have to import the respective test modules.

For example, in the `ItemDetailsComponent` test spec, before running each test, we have to import those references:

```
  beforeEach(async () => {
    await TestBed.configureTestingModule({
      declarations: [ItemDetailsComponent],
      imports: [RouterModule.forRoot([])],
      providers: [
        provideHttpClient(),
        provideHttpClientTesting()
      ]
    })
    .compileComponents();

    fixture = TestBed.createComponent(ItemDetailsComponent);
    component = fixture.componentInstance;
    fixture.detectChanges();
  });
```

LISTING 18-1: item-details.component.spec.ts

For services, we will have to add the following providers:

```
  beforeEach(() => {
    TestBed.configureTestingModule({
      providers: [
        provideHttpClient(),
        provideHttpClientTesting()
      ]
    });
    service = TestBed.inject(AuthenticationService);
  });
```

LISTING 18-2: authentication.service.spec.ts

In the components where we use forms, the import of the Forms and ReactiveForms module will also be required:

```
beforeEach(async () => {
  await TestBed.configureTestingModule({
    declarations: [LoginComponent],
    imports: [RouterModule.forRoot([]),
      ReactiveFormsModule],
    providers: [
      provideHttpClient(),
      provideHttpClientTesting()
    ]
  })
  .compileComponents();

  fixture = TestBed.createComponent(LoginComponent);
  component = fixture.componentInstance;
  fixture.detectChanges();
});
```

LISTING 18-3: login.component.spec.ts

We also have to add imports for pagination:

```
beforeEach(async () => {
  await TestBed.configureTestingModule({
    declarations: [ItemsComponent],
    imports: [RouterModule.forRoot([]),
      FormsModule,
      NgbPagination],
    providers: [
      provideHttpClient(),
      provideHttpClientTesting()
    ]
  })
  .compileComponents();

  fixture = TestBed.createComponent(ItemsComponent);
  component = fixture.componentInstance;
  fixture.detectChanges();
});
```

LISTING 18-4: items.component.spec.ts

We will need to make the NgbActiveModal service available in the tests where a modal dialog is used (in the Filter and ErrorDialog components). This time we use the providers keyword:

```
  beforeEach(async () => {
    await TestBed.configureTestingModule({
      declarations: [FilterComponent],
      imports: [RouterModule.forRoot([]),
      FormsModule],
      providers: [
        provideHttpClient(),
        provideHttpClientTesting(),
        NgbActiveModal
      ]
    })
    .compileComponents();

    fixture = TestBed.createComponent(FilterComponent);
    component = fixture.componentInstance;
    fixture.detectChanges();
  });
```

LISTING 18-5: filter.component.spec.ts

Finally, we should add imports for the reCAPTCHA modules in the registration component:

```
  beforeEach(async () => {
    await TestBed.configureTestingModule({
      declarations: [RegistrationComponent],
      imports: [RouterModule.forRoot([]),
        ReactiveFormsModule,
        RecaptchaFormsModule,
        RecaptchaModule],
      providers: [
        provideHttpClient(),
        provideHttpClientTesting()
      ]
    })
    .compileComponents();

    fixture = TestBed.createComponent(RegistrationComponent);
    component = fixture.componentInstance;
    fixture.detectChanges();
  });
```

LISTING 18-6: registration.component.spec.ts

We will also remove the tests from *analytics.directive.spec.ts* so that we can make all our tests run. We will come back to it in the next chapter.

After we have made those additions to our test files, we see that all tests pass successfully. Now we are ready to add our own tests!

Testing Components

We will start with testing the Items component. We want to make sure that the following functionality works:

- Updating page when the number products per page changes
- Updating page when the filter changes
- Changing pages with navigation toolbar
- Viewing a product and returning back to the same page (should preserve page number)

Let's see the first test case in full:

```
describe('ItemsComponent items per page', () => {
  let component: ItemsComponent;
  let fixture: ComponentFixture<ItemsComponent>;

  beforeEach(async () => {

    let testItems1: ItemPayload = {
      count: 14,
      items: [
        { id: 1, name: "a1", price: 1, category: "", description: "" },
        { id: 2, name: "a2", price: 1, category: "", description: "" },
        { id: 3, name: "a3", price: 1, category: "", description: "" }
      ]
    };
    let testItems2: ItemPayload = {
      count: 14,
      items: [
        { id: 1, name: "a1", price: 1, category: "", description: "" },
        { id: 2, name: "a2", price: 1, category: "", description: "" },
        { id: 3, name: "a3", price: 1, category: "", description: "" },
        { id: 4, name: "a4", price: 1, category: "", description: "" },
        { id: 5, name: "a5", price: 1, category: "", description: "" }
      ]
    };
    const itemService = jasmine.createSpyObj('ItemService', ['getItems']);
    const getItemsSpy
      = itemService.getItems.and.returnValues(of(testItems1), of(testItems2));

    await TestBed.configureTestingModule({
      declarations: [ItemsComponent],
      imports: [RouterModule.forRoot([]),
        FormsModule,
        NgbPagination],
      providers: [
        provideHttpClient(),
        provideHttpClientTesting(),
        { provide: ItemService, useValue: itemService }
      ]
    })
      .compileComponents();
  });
```

```
  beforeEach(() => {
    fixture = TestBed.createComponent(ItemsComponent);
    component = fixture.componentInstance;
    fixture.detectChanges();
  });

  it('should create', () => {
    expect(component).toBeTruthy();
  });

  it('should initially show 3 items', () => {
    let el = fixture.nativeElement.querySelectorAll('.card');
    expect(el.length).toEqual(3);
  });

  it('should show 5 items after page size change', () => {
    let el = fixture.nativeElement.querySelectorAll('.card');
    expect(el.length)
      .withContext('starting with 3 items')
      .toEqual(3);

    const select: HTMLSelectElement
      = fixture.nativeElement.querySelector('#pageSize');
    select.value = select.options[1].value;  // select a new value (5)
    select.dispatchEvent(new Event('change'));
    fixture.detectChanges();

    el = fixture.nativeElement.querySelectorAll('.card');
    expect(el.length)
      .withContext('finishing with 5 items')
      .toEqual(5);
    expect(component.storeService.page).toEqual(1);
  });
});
```

LISTING 18-7: items.component.spec.ts

Before running the three test cases, we need to mock the ItemService that this component depends on. For this, we use Jasmine's createSpyObj function. Here, we choose to spy on getItems function from ItemService. More specifically, we give the instructions that this function will be called two times. On the first time, an array of 3 items will be returned, while on the second time there will be 5 items. This is what ItemService will return after we use the drop-down element to change the page size from 3 to 5 items per page.

Our tests can gain access to the component DOM with the use of the nativeElement property of the created component. Here, we use functions querySelection() and querySelectionAll() with CSS selectors (#pageSize and .card) to get access to the page size drop-down and the item cards respectively.

With regard to the drop-down element, we select a new value (5 items per page) and we dispatch the change event. Afterwards, we call `detectChanges()` to trigger a change detection cycle. Then, we verify that our component indeed displays 5 items on the page.

Another interesting test case is the page filter change:

```
describe('ItemsComponent filter change', () => {
  let component: ItemsComponent;
  let fixture: ComponentFixture<ItemsComponent>;

  beforeEach(async () => {
    let testItems1: ItemPayload = {
      count: 14,
      items: [
        { id: 1, name: "a1", price: 1, category: "shoes", description: "" },
        { id: 2, name: "a2", price: 1, category: "clothes", description: "" },
        { id: 3, name: "a3", price: 1, category: "shoes", description: "" }
      ]
    };
    let testItems2: ItemPayload = {
      count: 14,
      items: [
        { id: 11, name: "b1", price: 1, category: "", description: "" },
        { id: 12, name: "b2", price: 1, category: "", description: "" },
        { id: 13, name: "b3", price: 1, category: "", description: "" }
      ]
    };
    let testItems3: ItemPayload = {
      count: 5,
      items: [
        { id: 1, name: "a1", price: 1, category: "shoes", description: "" },
        { id: 3, name: "a3", price: 1, category: "shoes", description: "" },
        { id: 4, name: "a4", price: 1, category: "shoes", description: "" }
      ]
    };
    const itemService = jasmine.createSpyObj('ItemService', ['getItems']);
    let getItemsSpy
      = itemService.getItems.and.returnValues(of(testItems1),
        of(testItems2), of(testItems3));

    await TestBed.configureTestingModule({
      declarations: [ItemsComponent],
      imports: [RouterModule.forRoot([]),
        FormsModule,
        NgbPagination],
      providers: [
        provideHttpClient(),
        provideHttpClientTesting(),
        { provide: ItemService, useValue: itemService }
      ]
    })
      .compileComponents();
  });

  beforeEach(() => {
```

```
    fixture = TestBed.createComponent(ItemsComponent);
    component = fixture.componentInstance;
    fixture.detectChanges();
  });

  it('should show go to first page after filter change', () => {
    component.onPageChange(3);
    fixture.detectChanges();
    expect(component.storeService.page).toEqual(3);

    const newFilter: Filter = { name: "", categories: ["shoes"] };
    component.storeService.filter = newFilter;
    fixture.detectChanges();
    const el = fixture.nativeElement.querySelectorAll('.card');

    expect(component.storeService.page).toEqual(1);
  });

});
```

LISTING 18-8: items.component.spec.ts

Here, the ItemService spy object is set to return 3 times:

- After we load the component
- After we change to page 3
- After we change the filter

We change the filter by setting the filter object in StoreService. As a result, we should check that we return to the first page as expected.

A sidenote about StoreService: one would expect to mock also this service, as we did with ItemService. However, there is no use mocking it, as it does not contain any important functionality (being a mere collection of BehaviorSubject objects).

Now, let's move to the ItemDetailsComponent. The test cases here are much simpler, but we will also see them as they include route testing functionality:

```
describe('ItemDetailsComponent', () => {
  let component: ItemDetailsComponent;
  let fixture: ComponentFixture<ItemDetailsComponent>;
  let route: ActivatedRoute;

  beforeEach(async () => {

    let testItem = {
      id: 1, name: "a1", price: 1, category: "",
      description: ""
    };
    const itemService = jasmine.createSpyObj('ItemService', ['getItem']);
    let getItemsSpy = itemService.getItem.and.returnValue(of(testItem));
```

```
    await TestBed.configureTestingModule({
      declarations: [ItemDetailsComponent],
      imports: [RouterModule.forRoot([])],
      providers: [
        provideHttpClient(),
        provideHttpClientTesting(),
        { provide: ItemService, useValue: itemService }
      ]
    })
    .compileComponents();

    fixture = TestBed.createComponent(ItemDetailsComponent);
    component = fixture.componentInstance;
    fixture.detectChanges();
  });

  beforeEach(() => {
    route = TestBed.inject(ActivatedRoute);
    spyOn(route.snapshot.paramMap, 'get').and.returnValue('1'); //itemID = 1

    fixture = TestBed.createComponent(ItemDetailsComponent);
    component = fixture.componentInstance;
    fixture.detectChanges();
  });

  it('should create', () => {
    expect(component).toBeTruthy();
  });

  it('should display selected item', () => {
    expect(component.item.name).toEqual('a1');
  });

  it('should add item to cart and navigate to cart page',
    inject([Router], (router: Router) => {
    spyOn(router, 'navigate').and.stub();

    const addToCartButton: HTMLElement
      = fixture.debugElement.query(By.css('#addToCart')).nativeElement;
    addToCartButton.dispatchEvent(new Event('click'));
    fixture.detectChanges();
    expect(component.storeService.cart.cartItems.length).toEqual(1);
    expect(router.navigate).toHaveBeenCalledWith(['/cart']);
  }));
});
```

LISTING 19-6: item.component.spec.ts

The new stuff here is Jasmine's `spyOn` function that we use in two places:

First of all, we use it to mock the `paramMap` property of the route snapshot, so that it returns the correct ID of the item to be displayed in the newly created component.

Then, we use it to mock the `navigate` function of the router object. Note that the actual function is not called eventually (by using: `.and.stub`).

In the third and more interesting case, we can see another way of getting access to the `nativeElement` property. We use the `debugElement` property of the component, which wraps the native elements of the component. A reason to use this would be that we happen to run our tests in a non-browser platform. As long as we run our tests through a browser, we are ok to access the `nativeElement` property directly.

At the end of the test, we can verify that the item has been inserted into the cart and that we navigate to the cart details page.

In the next article, we will continue with the unit testing scenarios. You may find the code for this chapter here:

https://github.com/htset/eshop-angular-18/tree/part18

19. Angular testing – part 2

In this chapter, we will continue with frontend testing. We will see how to test complex components and asynchronous operations. We will also delve into services and interceptors testing.

Testing complex components

Components may have a complex structure, with a variety of @if expressions that control how it will be rendered. Furthermore, it may contain one or more nested components.

For this demonstration we will use CheckoutComponent, as it is rather complicated, and it also contains a nested component (DeliveryAddressComponent).

First of all, we want to verify that the component is rendered correctly. The appearance of the component depends on the following:

- whether the user is logged in or not
- whether a delivery address has been already stored for this user
- whether the cart is empty or not

The following snippet depicts the case where a user has been logged in, and has already entered a delivery address in the past:

```
beforeEach(async () => {
  await TestBed.configureTestingModule({
    declarations: [CheckoutComponent, DummyChildComponent],
    imports: [RouterModule.forRoot([]),
      FormsModule],
    providers: [
      provideHttpClient(),
      provideHttpClientTesting(),
      {
        provide: AuthenticationService,
        useClass: AuthenticationServiceStub
      }
    ]
  })
    .compileComponents();
});

beforeEach(() => {
  fixture = TestBed.createComponent(CheckoutComponent);
  component = fixture.componentInstance;
  component.storeService.user = new User(); //authenticated user
  component.storeService.user.id = 1;
  component.storeService.cart.emptyCart();
});

it('should show empty cart and one address', () => {
  spyOn(component.userService, 'getAddressByUserId')
```

```
      .and.returnValue(of([testAddress1]));
    fixture.detectChanges();
    expect(fixture.debugElement.query(By.css("#cartBody")))
      .withContext('cartBody')
      .toBeNull();
    expect(fixture.debugElement.query(By.css("#noCartBody")).nativeElement)
      .withContext('noCartBody')
      .toBeTruthy();
    expect(fixture.debugElement.query(By.css("#addressBody")).nativeElement)
      .withContext('addressBody')
      .toBeTruthy();
    expect(fixture.debugElement.query(By.css("#loginLink")))
      .withContext('loginLink')
      .toBeNull();
    expect(component.storeService.deliveryAddress)
      .toEqual(-1);
    expect(fixture.debugElement
      .queryAll(By.css('input[name="selectedAddress"]')).length)
      .withContext('addresses table')
      .toEqual(2);
    expect(fixture.debugElement
      .queryAll(By.css('input[name="selectedAddress"]:checked')).length)
      .toEqual(0);
});
```

LISTING 19-1: checkout.component.spec.ts

To make those tests run, we have to create the `AuthenticationServiceStub` class in a new folder called mocks:

```
import { BehaviorSubject, of } from 'rxjs';
import { User } from '../models/user';

let testUser: User =
{
  id: 1,
  username: 'test',
  password: '',
  firstName: 'Test',
  lastName: 'user',
  token: '',
  role: 'admin',
  email: 'test@test.com'
};

export class AuthenticationServiceStub {

  public get currentUserValue(): User {
    let currentUserSubject: BehaviorSubject<User>
      = new BehaviorSubject<User>(testUser);
    return currentUserSubject.value;
  }
```

}

LISTING 19-2: authentication.service.mock.ts

Note that, before each test, we call the `empty()` function of the cart in order to delete the cart contents in the store service, and most importantly, in the session storage.

Testing nested components

Now, we would like to test how `CheckoutComponent` interacts with `DeliveryAddressComponent`. This component receives a predefined address as input and emits an `addresssChangedEvent` with the newly edited address as output.

We can test this interaction by creating a dymmy child component that will implement only the input and output of `DeliveryAddressComponent`:

```
@Component({ selector: 'app-delivery-address', template: '{{address}}' })
class DummyChildComponent {
  address = model<Address>();

  ngOnInit() {
    console.log('on dummy init');
    console.log(this.address);
  }
  onDummySubmit() {
    console.log('on dummy submit');
    console.log(this.address);
    this.address.set(modifiedTestAddress);
  }
}
```

LISTING 19-3: checkout.component.spec.ts

In our tests, we verify that the nested dummy component gets rendered when we select to modify an existing address. We also test whether this address is correctly refreshed upon modification in the dummy component:

```
describe('CheckoutComponent delivery address', () => {
  let component: CheckoutComponent;
  let fixture: ComponentFixture<CheckoutComponent>;

  beforeEach(async () => {
    await TestBed.configureTestingModule({
      declarations: [CheckoutComponent, DummyChildComponent],
      imports: [RouterModule.forRoot([]),
        FormsModule],
      providers: [
        provideHttpClient(),
        provideHttpClientTesting(),
        {
```

```
          provide: AuthenticationService,
          useClass: AuthenticationServiceStub
        }
      ]
    })
      .compileComponents();
}));

beforeEach(() => {
  fixture = TestBed.createComponent(CheckoutComponent);
  component = fixture.componentInstance;
  component.storeService.user = new User(); //authenticated user
  component.storeService.user.id = 1;
});

it('should be editable after Modify button click', () => {
  component.storeService.cart.cartItems = [{ item: testItem, quantity: 1 }];
  spyOn(component.userService, 'getAddressByUserId')
    .and.returnValue(of([testAddress1]));
  fixture.detectChanges();
  expect(component.storeService.deliveryAddress)
    .toEqual(-1);
  expect(fixture.debugElement.nativeElement
    .querySelector('app-delivery-address'))
    .toBeNull();

  let el: HTMLButtonElement = fixture.debugElement
    .query(By.css('#modify1')).nativeElement;
  el.dispatchEvent(new Event("click"));
  fixture.detectChanges();

  console.log(fixture.debugElement
    .query(By.css('app-delivery-address')));
  console.log(fixture.debugElement.nativeElement
    .querySelector('app-delivery-address'));
  expect(fixture.debugElement.nativeElement
    .querySelector('app-delivery-address')).not.toBeNull();
});

it('should refresh address after modification', () => {
  component.storeService.cart.cartItems = [{ item: testItem, quantity: 1 }];
  let spy = spyOn(component.userService, 'getAddressByUserId')
    .and.returnValues(of([testAddress1, testAddress2]));
  fixture.detectChanges();

  expect(component.storeService.deliveryAddress)
    .toEqual(-1);
  expect(fixture.debugElement.nativeElement
    .querySelector('app-delivery-address'))
    .toBeNull();

  let el: HTMLButtonElement = fixture.debugElement
    .query(By.css('#modify1')).nativeElement;
  el.dispatchEvent(new Event("click"));
  fixture.detectChanges();
```

```
      expect(fixture.debugElement.query(By.css('#modify1')))
        .toBeNull();
      expect(fixture.debugElement.query(By.css('#cancel1')).nativeElement)
        .toBeTruthy();

      //we do NOT create the child - it is created by the host component
      //we just access it
      let childFixture = fixture.debugElement
        .query(By.directive(DummyChildComponent));
      let childComponent = childFixture.componentInstance;

      console.log(fixture.debugElement
        .query(By.directive(DummyChildComponent)));
      console.log(fixture.debugElement
        .query(By.css('app-delivery-address')));
      console.log(fixture.debugElement.nativeElement.
        querySelector('app-delivery-address'));
      expect(fixture.debugElement.nativeElement
        .querySelector('app-delivery-address')).not.toBeNull();

      //'getAddressByUserId' will be called again (now with the modified address)
      spy.and.returnValues(of([modifiedTestAddress, testAddress2]));
      let spy2 = spyOn(component.userService, 'saveAddress')
        .and.returnValues(of(modifiedTestAddress));

      childComponent.onDummySubmit();
      fixture.detectChanges();

      expect(fixture.debugElement
        .query(By.css('#addressBody form table')).nativeElement.innerHTML)
        .toContain('tt-new');
      expect(fixture.debugElement
        .query(By.css('#modify1')).nativeElement)
        .toBeTruthy();
      expect(fixture.debugElement
        .query(By.css('#cancel1')))
        .toBeNull();
   });
});
```

LISTING 19-4: checkout.component.spec.ts

Testing asynchronous operations

Another interesting test case is the following scenario (again in `CheckoutComponent`):

- the user has selected a delivery address
- leaves the page (e.g. goes back to the cart)
- returns to the checkout page

In this case, the delivery address ID will have already been set in the store service when the component loads for the second time:

```
it('should have radio box checked if address has already been selected before',
fakeAsync(() => {
  spyOn(component.userService, 'getAddressByUserId')
    .and.returnValue(of([testAddress1, testAddress2]));
  component.storeService.deliveryAddress = 2;
  fixture.detectChanges();
  tick();
  expect(component.storeService.deliveryAddress).toEqual(2);
  expect(fixture.debugElement
    .queryAll(By.css('input[name="selectedAddress"]')).length)
    .withContext('addresses table')
    .toEqual(3);
  expect(fixture.debugElement
    .queryAll(By.css('input[name="selectedAddress"]:checked')).length)
    .toEqual(1);
  console.log(fixture.debugElement
    .queryAll(By.css('input[name="selectedAddress"]:checked')));
}));
```

LISTING 19-5: checkout.component.spec.ts

This test case will fail, because the checked radio boxes will be 0 instead of 1. By examining the component's template, we see that we use `ngModel` to set the initial value of the radio boxes:

```
<input type="radio"
       id="selectedAddress{{addr.id}}"
       name="selectedAddress"
       [value]="addr.id"
       [ngModel]="selectedAddressId()"
       (change)="selectionChanged($any($event.target).id)"/>
```

LISTING 19-6: checkout.component.html

It turns out that `ngModel` is asynchronous, and it will take some time to update the values of the radio boxes, after changing the delivery address ID. This is why no radio box is checked at the time of the expectations checking.

We can solve this problem with the use of `fakeAsync`:

```
it('should have radio box checked if address has already been selected before',
fakeAsync(() => {
  spyOn(component.userService, 'getAddressByUserId')
    .and.returnValue(of([testAddress1, testAddress2]));
  component.storeService.deliveryAddress = 2;
  fixture.detectChanges();
  tick();
  expect(component.storeService.deliveryAddress).toEqual(2);
```

```
    expect(fixture.debugElement
      .queryAll(By.css('input[name="selectedAddress"]')).length)
      .withContext('addresses table')
      .toEqual(3);
    expect(fixture.debugElement
      .queryAll(By.css('input[name="selectedAddress"]:checked')).length)
      .toEqual(1);
    console.log(fixture.debugElement
      .queryAll(By.css('input[name="selectedAddress"]:checked')));
}));
```

LISTING 19-7: checkout.component.spec.ts

When we wrap our test function in `fakeAsync` we can take control of time and simulate it as we wish. By using `tick()` after change detection, we allow for sufficient time to pass, so that all changes have been detected before we move to the expectations.

Now that we know about testing asynchronous operations, a question: why we did not use `fakeAsync` also in the case of events? The answer is that `dispatchEvent()` evokes event handles synchronously, so there is no need for asynchronous testing.

Testing services

In this project, nearly all services are quite simple: they call the backend using `HttpClient` and they just return an Observable. The only case where the service contains a bit of functionality is in `AuthenticationService`, where the `User` object is stored in the session storage. Here, we will test the login process:

```
describe('AuthenticationService', () => {
  let authService: AuthenticationService;
  let storeService: StoreService;
  let httpTestingController: HttpTestingController;
  let expectedUser: User = { username: "usr", password: "passwd" };

  beforeEach(() => {
    TestBed.configureTestingModule({
      providers: [
        provideHttpClient(),
        provideHttpClientTesting()
      ]
    });
    authService = TestBed.inject(AuthenticationService);
    storeService = TestBed.inject(StoreService);
    httpTestingController = TestBed.inject(HttpTestingController);

    sessionStorage.removeItem('user');
    storeService.user = null;
  });

  it('should be created', () => {
    expect(authService).toBeTruthy();
```

```
  });

  it("should login user with correct credentials", () => {
    authService.login("usr", "passwd")
      .subscribe((user) => {
        expect(user).toEqual(expectedUser);
        expect(sessionStorage.getItem('user'))
          .toEqual(JSON.stringify(expectedUser));
        expect(storeService.user).toEqual(expectedUser);
      });

    const req = httpTestingController
      .expectOne(`${environment.apiUrl}/users/authenticate`);
    expect(req.request.method).toEqual('POST');

    req.flush(expectedUser);
  });

  it("should return error when logging in with incorrect credentials", () => {
    let expectedBadRequest = { message: "Log in failed" };
    authService.login("usr", "wrong_passwd")
      .subscribe({
        error: (e) => {
          expect(e.status).toEqual(400);
          expect(sessionStorage.getItem('user')).toBeNull();
          expect(storeService.user).toBeNull();
        }
      });

    const req = httpTestingController
      .expectOne(`${environment.apiUrl}/users/authenticate`);
    expect(req.request.method).toEqual('POST');

    req.flush(expectedBadRequest, { status: 400, statusText: 'bad request' });
  });
});
```

LISTING 19-8: authentication.service.spec.ts

For the tests, we use the `HttpTestingController`. We inject the `AuthenticationService` object and we use it to call `login()` function and test our expectations. We mock the HTTP response so that it contains the appropriate results.

Testing interceptors

The process of interceptor testing resembles that of service testing. Here we will see how to test the interceptor that adds a token in every outgoing request to the backend (*jwt.interceptor.ts*).

During test setup, we have to provide the interceptor to the testing module. We also inject the `ItemService`, as we will use it to make authenticated requests to the API:

```
describe('HttpInterceptorService', () => {
  let itemService: ItemService;
  let storeService: StoreService;
  let httpTestingController: HttpTestingController;

  beforeEach(() => {
    TestBed.configureTestingModule({
      imports: [HttpClientTestingModule],
      providers: [
        { provide: HTTP_INTERCEPTORS, useClass: JwtInterceptor, multi: true },
      ]
    });
    itemService = TestBed.inject(ItemService);
    storeService = TestBed.inject(StoreService);
    httpTestingController = TestBed.inject(HttpTestingController);
  });

  it('should insert token for logged in users', () => {
    let testItem = {
      id: 1, name: "a1", price: 1,
      category: "", description: ""
    };
    storeService.user = new User();
    storeService.user.token = "test_token";

    itemService.getItem(1)
      .subscribe();

    const req = httpTestingController.expectOne(r =>
      r.headers.has('Authorization')
        && r.headers.get('Authorization') === 'Bearer test_token');

    req.flush(testItem);
  });

  it('should not insert token for non-logged in users', () => {
    let testItem = {
      id: 1, name: "a1", price: 1,
      category: "", description: ""
    };
    storeService.user = null;

    itemService.getItem(1)
      .subscribe();

    const req = httpTestingController.expectOne(r =>
      !r.headers.has('Authorization'));

    req.flush(testItem);
  });
})
```

LISTING 19-9: jwt.interceptor.spec.ts

In both test cases, we check whether the request headers contain the token or not.

Directives testing

Finally, we will see how to test our directive. We will create a test component and will apply the directive to this:

```
@Component({
  template: `<input type="button"
             id="test" value="Test"
             appAnalytics events="click" />`
})
class TestComponent {
}

describe('AnalyticsDirective', () => {
  let component: TestComponent;
  let fixture: ComponentFixture<TestComponent>;
  let originalLog: any;

  beforeEach(async () => {
    await TestBed.configureTestingModule({
      declarations: [AnalyticsDirective
        , TestComponent],
    })
      .compileComponents();

    fixture = TestBed.createComponent(TestComponent);
    component = fixture.componentInstance;
    fixture.detectChanges();

    originalLog = console.log;
    spyOn(console, 'log');
  });

  afterEach(() => {
    // Restore the original console.log after each test
    console.log = originalLog;
  });

  it('should create an instance', () => {
    let el: HTMLButtonElement = fixture.debugElement
      .query(By.css('#test')).nativeElement;
    el.dispatchEvent(new Event("click"));
    fixture.detectChanges();

    expect(console.log).toHaveBeenCalled();
    expect(console.log).toHaveBeenCalledWith("Event: click");
  });
});
```

LISTING 19-10: analytics.directive.spec.ts

You can find more test cases about other components, such as CartComponent, DeliveryAddressComponent and ItemService in the code here:

https://github.com/htset/eshop-angular-18/tree/part19

20. ASP.NET Core Web API testing

We will conclude this book, with some unit testing on the backend side. We will test the `UserController` class, as it contains a more complex functionality, compared to the other controllers.

In unit testing, we test each class in isolation, and we mock all external dependencies. `UserController` class contains a reference to `EshopContext` class, which is difficult to mock. To solve this, we choose to move all database handling functionality to a new class, called `UserService`. This class will implement a new interface (`IUserService`) that will be injected into our controller:

```
using eshop_angular_18.Server.Models;

namespace eshop_angular_18.Server.Services
{
  public interface IUserService
  {
    public Task<List<User>> GetUsers();
    public Task<User?> GetUserById(int id);
    public Task<User?> GetUserByUsername(string? username);
    public Task<User?> GetUserByEmail(string? email);
    public Task<User?> GetUserByRegistrationCode(string? code);
    public Task<User?> GetUserFromTokens(string? token, string? refreshToken);
    public Task<User?> GetUserFromRefreshToken(string? refreshToken);
    public Task CreateUser(User user);
    public Task UpdateUser(User user);
  }
}
```

LISTING 20-1 IUserService.cs

This interface contains all the operations that our controller will need, in order to get information about users from the database, like finding users based on their ID, email, or username.

Class `UserService` implements the `IUserService` interface:

```
using eshop_angular_18.Server.Models;
using Microsoft.EntityFrameworkCore;

namespace eshop_angular_18.Server.Services
{
  public class UserService : IUserService
  {
    private readonly EshopContext Context;

    public UserService(EshopContext context)
    {
      Context = context;
```

```csharp
    }

    public async Task<List<User>> GetUsers()
    {
      return await Context.Users
          .Select(x => new User()
          {
            Id = x.Id,
            FirstName = x.FirstName,
            LastName = x.LastName,
            Username = x.Username,
            Password = null,
            Role = x.Role,
            Email = x.Email
          })
          .ToListAsync();
    }

    public async Task<User?> GetUserById(int id)
    {
      return await Context.Users.FindAsync(id);
    }

    public async Task<User?> GetUserByUsername(string? username)
    {
      return await Context.Users
          .SingleOrDefaultAsync(x => x.Username == username);
    }

    public async Task<User?> GetUserByEmail(string? email)
    {
      return await Context.Users
          .SingleOrDefaultAsync(x => x.Email == email);
    }

    public async Task<User?> GetUserByRegistrationCode(string? code)
    {
      return await Context.Users
          .SingleOrDefaultAsync(u => u.RegistrationCode == code);
    }

    public async Task<User?>
      GetUserFromTokens(string? token, string? refreshToken)
    {
      return await Context.Users
          .SingleOrDefaultAsync(u => (u.RefreshToken == refreshToken)
              && (u.Token == token));
    }

    public async Task<User?> GetUserFromRefreshToken(string? refreshToken)
    {
      return await Context.Users
          .SingleOrDefaultAsync(u => (u.RefreshToken == refreshToken));
    }
```

```
    public async Task CreateUser(User user)
    {
      await Context.Users.AddAsync(user);
      await Context.SaveChangesAsync();
    }

    public async Task UpdateUser(User user)
    {
      Context.Users.Update(user);
      await Context.SaveChangesAsync();
    }
  }
}
```

LISTING 20-2: UserService.cs

Now, `UserController` class gets a reference to the `IUserService` interface and, uses it to call the methods that have been implemented in the concrete class (`UserService`):

```
using eshop_angular_18.Server.Helpers;
using eshop_angular_18.Server.Models;
using eshop_angular_18.Server.Services;
using Microsoft.AspNetCore.Authorization;
using Microsoft.AspNetCore.Cors;
using Microsoft.AspNetCore.Mvc;
using Microsoft.Extensions.Options;
using Microsoft.IdentityModel.Tokens;
using System.IdentityModel.Tokens.Jwt;
using System.Net.Mail;
using System.Security.Claims;
using System.Security.Cryptography;
using System.Text;
namespace my_eshop_api.Controllers
{
  //*******************
  //Helper classes
  //*******************

  public class RegistrationCode
  {
    public string? Code { get; set; }
  }

  public class ResetEmail
  {
    public string? Email { get; set; }
  }

  [Route("api/users")]
  [EnableCors("angular_eshop_AllowSpecificOrigins")]
  [ApiController]
  public class UserController : ControllerBase
  {
```

```csharp
private readonly IUserService Service;
private readonly AppSettings AppSettings;

public UserController(IUserService service,
    IOptions<AppSettings> appSettings)
{
  Service = service;
  AppSettings = appSettings.Value;
}

//*******************
//REST handlers
//*******************

[HttpPost("authenticate")]
public async Task<IActionResult> Authenticate([FromBody] User formParams)
{
  if (formParams == null || formParams.Username == null)
    return BadRequest(new { message = "Log in failed" });

  var user = await Service.GetUserByUsername(formParams.Username);

  if (user == null || user.Password == null)
    return BadRequest(new { message = "Log in failed" });

  if (!PasswordHasher.VerifyPassword(formParams.Password, user.Password))
    return BadRequest(new { message = "Log in failed" });

  if (user.Status != "Active")
    return BadRequest(new
    {
      message = "Registration has not been confirmed"
    });

  user.Token = CreateToken(user);
  user.RefreshToken = CreateRefreshToken();
  user.RefreshTokenExpiry = DateTime.Now.AddMinutes(2);
  await Service.UpdateUser(user);

  user.Password = null;

  return Ok(user);
}

[Authorize(Roles = "admin")]
[HttpGet]
public async Task<ActionResult<List<User>>> GetAllUsers()
{
  return await Service.GetUsers();
}

[Authorize]
[HttpGet("{id}")]
public async Task<ActionResult<User?>> GetUser(int id)
{
```

```csharp
    var user = await Service.GetUserById(id);
    if (user != null)
      user.Password = null;
    return user;
}

[HttpPost("refresh")]
public async Task<IActionResult> RefreshToken([FromBody] User data)
{
    var user = await Service.GetUserFromTokens(data.Token, data.RefreshToken);

    if (user == null || DateTime.Now > user.RefreshTokenExpiry)
      return BadRequest(new { message = "Invalid token" });

    user.Token = CreateToken(user);
    user.RefreshToken = CreateRefreshToken();
    user.RefreshTokenExpiry = DateTime.Now.AddDays(7);
    await Service.UpdateUser(user);

    user.Password = null;

    return Ok(user);
}

[Authorize]
[HttpPost("revoke")]
public async Task<IActionResult> RevokeToken([FromBody] User data)
{
    var user = await Service.GetUserFromRefreshToken(data.RefreshToken);

    if (user == null || DateTime.Now > user.RefreshTokenExpiry)
      return BadRequest(new { message = "Invalid token" });

    user.Token = null;
    user.RefreshToken = null;
    user.RefreshTokenExpiry = null;
    await Service.UpdateUser(user);

    user.Password = null;

    return Ok(user);
}

[HttpPost]
[AllowAnonymous]
public async Task<ActionResult<User>> Register([FromBody] User user)
{
    if ((await Service.GetUserByUsername(user.Username)) != null)
    {
      return BadRequest("Username is already used");
    }

    if ((await Service.GetUserByEmail(user.Email)) != null)
    {
      return BadRequest("Email is already used");
```

```csharp
    }
    user.Role = "customer";
    user.Password = PasswordHasher.HashPassword(user.Password);
    user.Status = "Pending";
    user.RegistrationCode = CreateConfirmationToken();

    await Service.CreateUser(user);

    SendConfirmationEmail(user);

    return CreatedAtAction(nameof(GetUser), new { id = user.Id }, user);
}

[HttpPost("confirm_registration")]
[AllowAnonymous]
public async Task<ActionResult<User>>
  ConfirmRegistration([FromBody] RegistrationCode code)
{
    var user = await Service.GetUserByRegistrationCode(code.Code);
    if (user == null)
    {
        return BadRequest("Registration code not found");
    }

    if (user.Status == "Active")
    {
        return BadRequest("User is already activated");
    }

    user.Status = "Active";
    user.Token = CreateToken(user);
    user.RefreshToken = CreateRefreshToken();
    user.RefreshTokenExpiry = DateTime.Now.AddDays(7);

    await Service.UpdateUser(user);

    user.Password = null;

    return Ok(user);
}

[HttpPost("reset_password")]
[AllowAnonymous]
public async Task<ActionResult<User>>
  ResetPassword([FromBody] ResetEmail resetEmail)
{
    var user = await Service.GetUserByEmail(resetEmail.Email);
    if (user == null)
    {
        return BadRequest("Email not found");
    }

    user.Status = "PasswordReset";
    user.Password = null;
```

```csharp
    user.RegistrationCode = CreateConfirmationToken();

    await Service.UpdateUser(user);

    SendPasswordResetEmail(user);

    return Ok(user);
}

[HttpPost("change_password")]
[AllowAnonymous]
public async Task<ActionResult<User>>
 ChangePassword([FromBody] User inputUser)
{
    var user
       = await Service.GetUserByRegistrationCode(inputUser.RegistrationCode);

    if (user == null)
    {
        return BadRequest("User not found");
    }

    user.Password = PasswordHasher.HashPassword(inputUser.Password);
    user.Status = "Active";
    user.Token = CreateToken(user);
    user.RefreshToken = CreateRefreshToken();
    user.RefreshTokenExpiry = DateTime.Now.AddDays(7);

    await Service.UpdateUser(user);

    user.Password = null;

    return Ok(user);
}

//*******************
//private functions
//*******************

private string CreateToken(User user)
{
    var jwtTokenHandler = new JwtSecurityTokenHandler();
    var key = Encoding.ASCII.GetBytes(AppSettings.Secret);
    var identity = new ClaimsIdentity(new Claim[]
        {
                    new Claim(ClaimTypes.Role, user.Role)
        });
    var credentials =
        new SigningCredentials(new SymmetricSecurityKey(key),
            SecurityAlgorithms.HmacSha256);

    var tokenDescriptor = new SecurityTokenDescriptor
    {
        Subject = identity,
        Expires = DateTime.Now.AddMinutes(2),
```

```csharp
      SigningCredentials = credentials
    };

    var token = jwtTokenHandler.CreateToken(tokenDescriptor);
    return jwtTokenHandler.WriteToken(token);
}

private string CreateRefreshToken()
{
    var randomNum = new byte[64];
    using (var generator = RandomNumberGenerator.Create())
    {
        generator.GetBytes(randomNum);
        return Convert.ToBase64String(randomNum);
    }
}
private string CreateConfirmationToken()
{
    var randomNum = new byte[64];
    using (var generator = RandomNumberGenerator.Create())
    {
        generator.GetBytes(randomNum);
        var tempString = Convert.ToBase64String(randomNum);
        return tempString.Replace("\\", "")
           .Replace("+", "").Replace("=", "").Replace("/", "");
    }
}

private void SendConfirmationEmail(User user)
{
    var smtpClient = new SmtpClient()
    {
        Host = AppSettings.SmtpHost,
        Port = AppSettings.SmtpPort,
        Credentials = new System.Net
          .NetworkCredential(AppSettings.SmtpUsername, AppSettings.SmtpPassword),
        EnableSsl = true
    };

    var message = new MailMessage()
    {
        From = new MailAddress("info@my-eshop.com"),
        Subject = "Confirm Registration",
        Body = "To confirm registration please click <a href=\"https://localhost:4200/confirm_registration?code=" + user.RegistrationCode + "\">here</a>",
        IsBodyHtml = true
    };

    message.To.Add(user.Email);

    //smtpClient.Send(message);
}

private void SendPasswordResetEmail(User user)
```

```
    {
        var smtpClient = new SmtpClient()
        {
            Host = AppSettings.SmtpHost,
            Port = AppSettings.SmtpPort,
            Credentials = new System.Net
                .NetworkCredential(AppSettings.SmtpUsername, AppSettings.SmtpPassword),
            EnableSsl = true
        };

        var message = new MailMessage()
        {
            From = new MailAddress("info@my-eshop.com"),
            Subject = "Email reset",
            Body = "To insert a new password, please click <a href=\"https://localhost:4200/new_password?code=" + user.RegistrationCode + "\">here</a>",
            IsBodyHtml = true
        };

        message.To.Add(user.Email);

        //smtpClient.Send(message);
    }

    }
}
```

LISTING 20-3: UserController.cs

We need to update *Program.cs*, so that a UserService object is injected into UserController:

builder.Services.AddScoped<IUserService, UserService>();

LISTING 20-4: PROGRAM.CS

Now we are ready to start testing! We will create a new NUnit Test Project and we will add it in the same solution. We have to add a new reference to the Web API project, so that its classes (i.e. UserController, User, and s.o.) are available in the test project. To do this, we right-click on the test project, then we select *Add -> Project Reference.*

In order to test the UserController functionality, we have two options:

- We can create a dummy UserService class that implements IUserService interface without using the database
- We can use a mocking framework, such as *Moq*, to mock the UserService class

We will go with the second option, and we will install Moq with NuGet. We then create a set of Unit Tests for the authenticate method:

using eshop_angular_18.Server.Helpers;

```csharp
using eshop_angular_18.Server.Models;
using eshop_angular_18.Server.Services;
using Microsoft.AspNetCore.Mvc;
using Microsoft.Extensions.Options;
using Moq;
using my_eshop_api.Controllers;

namespace eshop_angular_18.Server.tests
{
    public class Tests
    {
        AppSettings appSettings;
        User user;
        Mock<IUserService> mockService;
        UserController controller;

        [SetUp]
        public void Setup()
        {
            appSettings = new AppSettings()
            {
                Secret = "this is a very long string to be used as secret",
                SmtpHost = "smtp.host",
                SmtpPort = 587,
                SmtpUsername = "username@mysite.com",
                SmtpPassword = "passssss"
            };

            var iop = Options.Create(appSettings);

            user = new User()
            {
                Id = 1,
                FirstName = "a1",
                LastName = "b1",
                Username = "user1",
                Password = "Ln0g6rm/5ZZsk7aiTD4m+u04VvVttKlrTLtlsdUE1FeFdeoT",
                Email = "user1@gmail.com",
                Role = "admin",
                Status = "Active"
            };

            mockService = new Mock<IUserService>();
            controller = new UserController(mockService.Object, iop);

            mockService.Setup(s => s.GetUserByUsername("user1111"))
                .ReturnsAsync((User)null);
            mockService.Setup(s => s.GetUserByUsername("user1"))
                .ReturnsAsync(user);
            mockService.Setup(s => s.UpdateUser(It.IsAny<User>()));

        }

        [Test]
        public async Task WhenLoginFormIsNull_ReturnBadRequest()
```

```csharp
{
  User? testUser = null;

  var response = await controller.Authenticate(testUser)
      as BadRequestObjectResult;
  Assert.IsInstanceOf<BadRequestObjectResult>(response);
}

[Test]
public async Task WhenWrongUsername_ReturnBadRequest()
{
  var testUser = new User()
  {
    Username = "user1111",
    Password = "pass1"
  };

  var response = await controller.Authenticate(testUser)
      as BadRequestObjectResult;
  Assert.IsInstanceOf<BadRequestObjectResult>(response);
}

[Test]
public async Task WhenUserIsPending_ReturnBadRequest()
{
  user.Status = "Pending";

  var testUser = new User()
  {
    Username = "user1",
    Password = "user"
  };

  var response
    = await controller.Authenticate(testUser) as BadRequestObjectResult;
  Assert.IsInstanceOf<BadRequestObjectResult>(response);
}

[Test]
public async Task WhenCorrectCredentials_ReturnOK()
{
  var testUser = new User()
  {
    Username = "user1",
    Password = "user"
  };

  var response = await controller.Authenticate(testUser)
      as OkObjectResult;
  Assert.IsInstanceOf<OkObjectResult>(response);
  var model = response.Value as User;
  Assert.IsNotNull(model);
  Assert.IsNotNull(model.Token);
  Assert.IsNotNull(model.RefreshToken);
  Assert.IsNull(model.Password);
```

            }
        }
    }

LISTING 20-5: UnitTest1.cs

During test setup, we create a mock of the `UserService` class and we pass it as a parameter into `UserController`'s constructor. We also setup the mock service to return a null user when we use method `GetUserByUsername` with a wrong username. We also instruct it to return an actual `User` object when we use the correct username. Finally, we mock `UpdateUser` method to always succeed.

In the four displayed tests, we check for the following cases:

- `Authenticate()` is called with a null `User` object (the request had no parameters)
- A wrong username was used
- The correct login credentials were used, but the user had not yet confirmed his registration
- The correct login credentials were used, and the user had confirmed his registration

In the three first cases, we cast the response from the controller into a `BadRequestObjectResult`, while on the successful case we use the `OkObjectResult`. In the fourth case, we also get the returned `User` object, as it is updated by the controller and we check for the existence of the necessary tokens and that the returned password is indeed null.

In order to run the tests, we use the TestExplorer window (oprion View->Test Explorer).

You may find the code for this chapter here:

https://github.com/htset/eshop-angular-18/tree/part20

www.ingramcontent.com/pod-product-compliance
Lightning Source LLC
Chambersburg PA
CBHW062102220526
45471CB00010B/3576